Contents

Classroom Treats

peanut butter and jelly cookies

1 Butter Flavor CRISCO® Stick or 1 cup Butter Flavor CRISCO® all-vegetable shortening
1 cup JIF® Creamy Peanut Butter
1 teaspoon vanilla
⅔ cup firmly packed light brown sugar
⅓ cup granulated sugar
2 large eggs
2 cups all-purpose flour
1 cup SMUCKER'S® Strawberry Preserves or any flavor

1. Heat oven to 350°F.

2. Combine 1 cup shortening, peanut butter and vanilla in food processor fitted with metal blade. Process until well blended and smooth. Add sugars; process until incorporated completely. Add eggs; beat just until blended. Add flour; pulse until dough begins to form ball. *Do not overprocess.*

3. Place dough in medium bowl. Shape ½ tablespoon dough into ball for each cookie. Place 1½ inches apart on ungreased cookie sheets. Press thumb into center of each ball to create deep well. Fill each well with about ½ teaspoon preserves.

4. Bake at 350°F for 10 minutes or until lightly browned and firm. Cool on cookie sheets 4 minutes; transfer to cooling racks. Leave on racks about 30 minutes or until completely cool.

Makes about 5 dozen cookies

3

peanut butter and
jelly cookies

vanilla chocolate swirl ice cream cone cakes

¼ cup CRISCO® Stick or ¼ cup CRISCO® Shortening
¾ cup sugar
1 egg, slightly beaten
½ teaspoon vanilla
1 cup sifted cake flour
1 teaspoon baking powder
⅛ teaspoon salt
¼ cup milk
2 tablespoons cocoa powder
2 tablespoons mini chocolate chips
12 large flat-bottom ice cream cones
Buttery Cream Frosting (page 6)

Preheat oven to 350°F.

Beat CRISCO® Shortening and sugar vigorously by hand or at medium speed with electric mixer for 2 minutes. Add egg and vanilla; mix well.

Combine cake flour, baking powder and salt. Add to CRISCO® mixture alternately with milk, mixing thoroughly after each addition. Place half the batter in a separate bowl and stir in cocoa and mini chocolate chips. Mix with wooden spoon until well blended.

Divide the batters into cones, alternating chocolate and plain batter. Run a skewer through the batter once or twice to "swirl" the colors. Set cones in muffin cups or on a baking sheet. Bake for 25 to 30 minutes; cool.

Prepare Buttery Cream Frosting and frost cakes, or pipe on the frosting with a star tip in a circular pattern to create a "swirled" top. Decorate with assorted candies, sprinkles, coconut and marshmallows; top with a maraschino cherry.   *Makes 12 cone cakes*

continued on page 6

5

vanilla chocolate swirl ice cream cone cakes

vanilla chocolate swirl ice cream cone cakes, continued

buttery cream frosting

   4 cups confectioners' sugar
   ⅓ cup Butter Flavor CRISCO® All-Vegetable Shortening or ⅓ Butter Flavor CRISCO® Stick
   1½ teaspoons vanilla
   7 to 8 tablespoons milk

In medium mixing bowl, combine confectioners' sugar, Butter Flavor CRISCO® and vanilla. Slowly blend in milk to desired consistency. Beat on high speed for 5 minutes, or until smooth and creamy.

s'more bars

   1 package (18 ounces) refrigerated chocolate chip cookie dough
   ¼ cup graham cracker crumbs
   3 cups mini marshmallows
   ½ cup semisweet or milk chocolate chips
   2 teaspoons shortening

1. Preheat oven to 350°F. Grease 13×9×2-inch baking pan.

2. Remove dough from wrapper. Press dough into prepared pan. Sprinkle evenly with graham cracker crumbs.

3. Bake 10 to 12 minutes or until edges are golden brown. Sprinkle with marshmallows. Bake 2 to 3 minutes or until marshmallows are puffed. Cool completely on wire rack.

4. Combine chocolate chips and shortening in small resealable plastic food storage bag; seal. Microwave at HIGH (100% power) 1 minute; knead bag lightly. Microwave at HIGH for additional 30-second intervals until chips and shortening are completely melted and smooth, kneading bag after each 30-second interval. Cut off small corner of bag. Drizzle over bars. Refrigerate 5 to 10 minutes or until chocolate is set.   *Makes 3 dozen bars*

s'more bars

"radical" peanut butter pizza cookies

COOKIES
 1 Butter Flavor CRISCO® Stick or 1 cup Butter Flavor CRISCO® all-vegetable shortening
 1¼ cups granulated sugar, divided
 1 cup packed dark brown sugar
 1 cup JIF® Creamy Peanut Butter
 2 eggs
 1 teaspoon baking soda
 1 teaspoon vanilla
 ½ teaspoon salt
 2 cups all-purpose flour
 2 cups quick oats, uncooked

PIZZA SAUCE
 2 cups milk chocolate chips
 ¼ Butter Flavor CRISCO® Stick or ¼ cup Butter Flavor CRISCO® all-vegetable shortening

PIZZA TOPPINGS
 Recipes follow

DRIZZLE
 1 cup chopped white confectionery coating

1. Heat oven to 350°F. Place sheets of foil on countertop for cooling cookies.

2. For cookies, combine 1 cup shortening, 1 cup granulated sugar and brown sugar in large bowl. Beat at low speed of electric mixer until well blended. Add peanut butter, eggs, baking soda, vanilla and salt. Mix about 2 minutes or until well blended. Stir in flour and oats with spoon.

continued on page 10

9

"radical" peanut butter
pizza cookies

3. Place remaining ¼ cup granulated sugar in small bowl.

4. Measure ¼ cup dough. Shape into ball. Repeat with remaining dough. Roll each ball in sugar. Place 4 inches apart on ungreased cookie sheets. Flatten into 4-inch circles.

5. Bake at 350°F for 8 to 10 minutes. *Do not overbake.* Use back of spoon to flatten center and up to edge of each hot cookie to resemble pizza crust. Cool 5 to 8 minutes on baking sheet. Remove pizza to foil to cool completely.

6. For pizza sauce, combine chocolate chips and ¼ cup shortening in large microwave-safe measuring cup or bowl. Microwave at MEDIUM (50%) 2 to 3 minutes or until chips are shiny and soft (or melt on rangetop in small saucepan on very low heat). Stir until smooth. Spoon 2 teaspoons melted chocolate into center of each cookie. Spread to inside edge. Sprinkle desired toppings over chocolate.

7. For drizzle, place chopped confectionery coating in heavy resealable plastic food storage bag. Seal. Microwave at MEDIUM (50% power). Knead bag after 1 minute. Repeat until smooth (or melt by placing in bowl of hot water). Cut pinpoint hole in corner of bag. Squeeze out and drizzle over cookies. *Makes about 2 dozen cookies*

Pizza Toppings: **Mmmmm:** candy coated chocolate pieces **Beary good:** gummy bears **Jumbo jewels:** small pieces of gumdrops **Bubble gum-like:** round sprinkles and balls **German chocolate:** chopped pecans and flake coconut **Cherries jubilee:** candied cherries and slivered almonds **Rocky road:** miniature marshmallows and mini semisweet chocolate chips **Harvest mix:** candy corn and chopped peanuts **Ants and logs:** cashews and raisins

Tip: These cookies are a great project for kids' parties and rainy days. Premake the cookies and let each child create their own cookie pizza.

quick chocolate cupcakes

1½ cups all-purpose flour
¾ cup sugar
¼ cup HERSHEY'S Cocoa
1 teaspoon baking soda
½ teaspoon salt
1 cup water
¼ cup vegetable oil
1 tablespoon white vinegar
1 teaspoon vanilla extract
Chocolate Frosting (recipe follows)

1. Heat oven to 375°F. Line muffin cups (2½ inches in diameter) with paper baking cups.

2. Stir together flour, sugar, cocoa, baking soda and salt in medium bowl. Add water, oil, vinegar and vanilla; beat with whisk just until batter is smooth and ingredients are well blended. Fill muffin cups ⅔ full with batter.

3. Bake 16 to 18 minutes or until wooden pick inserted in center comes out clean. Remove from pans to wire racks. Cool completely. Prepare Chocolate Frosting; frost cupcakes.

Makes 14 cupcakes

chocolate frosting

3 tablespoons butter or margarine, softened
1 cup powdered sugar
¼ cup HERSHEY'S Cocoa
2 to 3 tablespoons milk
½ teaspoon vanilla extract

Beat butter in small bowl until creamy. Add powdered sugar and cocoa alternately with milk beating to spreading consistency. Stir in vanilla.

Makes about 1 cup frosting

shapers

2 packages (20 ounces each) refrigerated sugar cookie dough
   Red, yellow, green and blue paste food colorings
1 container (16 ounces) vanilla frosting

1. Remove dough from wrapper according to package directions. Cut each roll of dough in half.

2. Beat ¼ of dough and red food coloring in medium bowl until well blended. Shape red dough into 5-inch log on sheet of waxed paper; set aside.

3. Repeat with remaining dough and food colorings. Cover; refrigerate tinted logs 1 hour or until firm.

4. Roll or shape each log on smooth surface to create circular, triangular, square and oval-shaped logs. Use ruler to keep triangle and square sides flat. Cover; refrigerate dough 1 hour or until firm.

5. Preheat oven to 350°F. Cut shaped dough into ¼-inch slices. Place 2 inches apart on ungreased baking sheets. Bake 9 to 12 minutes. Remove to wire racks; cool completely.

6. Spoon frosting into resealable plastic food storage bag; seal. Cut tiny tip from corner of bag. Pipe frosting around each cookie to define shape.   *Makes about 6½ dozen cookies*

Tip

If you have extra liquid food colorings at home, tint the vanilla frosting different colors. Frost cookies using contrasting colored frosting, for example green frosting on a red cookie.

cookies & cream cupcakes

2¼ cups all-purpose flour
1 tablespoon baking powder
½ teaspoon salt
1⅔ cups sugar
1 cup milk
½ cup (1 stick) butter, softened
2 teaspoons vanilla
3 egg whites
1 cup crushed chocolate sandwich cookies (about 10 cookies) plus additional for garnish
1 container (16 ounces) vanilla frosting

1. Preheat oven to 350°F. Line 24 regular-size (2½-inch) muffin pan cups with paper baking cups.

2. Sift flour, baking powder and salt together in large bowl. Stir in sugar. Add milk, butter and vanilla; beat with electric mixer at low speed 30 seconds. Beat at medium speed 2 minutes. Add egg whites; beat 2 minutes. Stir in 1 cup crushed cookies.

3. Spoon batter into prepared muffin cups. Bake 20 to 25 minutes or until toothpicks inserted into centers come out clean. Cool in pans on wire racks 10 minutes. Remove to racks; cool completely.

4. Frost cupcakes; garnish with additional crushed cookies.   *Makes 24 cupcakes*

ooze cupcakes

1 package (8 ounces) cream cheese, softened
½ cup powdered sugar
⅓ cup frozen limeade concentrate, thawed
1 teaspoon vanilla
  Yellow and blue food coloring
1 package (18 ounces) chocolate cake mix
1 egg
  Water
  Vegetable oil
1 container (16 ounces) vanilla frosting
  Orange Halloween sugar sprinkles (optional)

1. Preheat oven to 350°F. Line 24 regular size (2½-inch) muffin pans with paper baking cups.

2. Beat cream cheese, powdered sugar, limeade concentrate and vanilla in medium bowl with electric mixer at medium speed. Mix in yellow food coloring by adding 1 drop at a time until desired color is reached; set aside.

3. Mix cake mix batter according to package directions using egg, water and oil. Fill baking cups half full with batter. Carefully place 1 rounded teaspoon cream cheese mixture in center of each.

4. Bake 20 minutes. Remove from oven and cool completely before frosting.

5. Add 4 drops yellow food coloring and 2 drops blue food coloring to frosting. Stir until well blended. Adjust color as needed by adding additional food coloring 1 drop at a time, blending well after each addition. Spread frosting onto cooled cupcakes. Top with sugar sprinkles, if desired.   *Makes 24 cupcakes*

surprise cookies

1 package (18 ounces) refrigerated sugar cookie dough
All-purpose flour (optional)
Any combination of walnut halves, whole almonds, chocolate-covered raisins or
  caramel candy squares for filling
Assorted colored sugars (optional)

1. Grease cookie sheets. Remove dough from wrapper according to package directions. Divide dough into 4 equal sections. Reserve 1 section; cover and refrigerate remaining 3 sections.

2. Roll out reserved dough to ¼-inch thickness. Sprinkle with flour to minimize sticking, if necessary. Cut out 3-inch square cookie with sharp knife. Transfer cookie to prepared cookie sheet.

3. Place desired "surprise" filling in center of cookie. (If using caramel candy square, place so that caramel forms diamond shape within square.)

4. Bring up 4 corners of dough towards center; pinch gently to seal. Repeat steps with remaining dough and fillings, placing cookies about 2 inches apart on prepared cookie sheets. Sprinkle with colored sugar, if desired. Freeze cookies 20 minutes. Meanwhile, preheat oven to 350°F.

5. Bake 9 to 11 minutes or until edges are lightly browned. Remove to wire racks; cool completely. *Makes about 14 cookies*

Tip: Make extra batches of these tasty cookies and store in freezer in heavy-duty freezer bags. Take out a few at a time for kids' after-school treats.

abc blocks

2 recipes Christmas Ornament Cookie Dough (page 22)
Red food coloring

1. Prepare 2 recipes Christmas Ornament Cookie Dough as directed. Tint one recipe dough to desired shade of red with food coloring. Wrap doughs separately in plastic wrap; refrigerate 30 minutes.

2. Shape ⅔ red dough into 1½×1½×6-inch square log, pressing log on sides to flatten. Shape ⅔ plain dough into 1½×1½×6-inch square log, pressing log on sides to flatten.

3. Roll remaining ⅓ red dough into 6×7-inch rectangle on waxed paper. Place plain log in center of red rectangle. Fold red edges up and around plain log. Press gently on top and sides of dough so entire log is wrapped in red dough. Flatten log slightly to form square log. Wrap log in plastic wrap; refrigerate 1 hour. Repeat process with remaining ⅓ plain dough and red log.

4. Preheat oven to 350°F. Lightly grease cookie sheets. Cut each log into same number of ¼-inch-thick slices. Place slices 1 inch apart on prepared cookie sheets. Using 1½-inch alphabet-shaped cookie cutters, cut out letter shapes from blocks, making sure to cut same number of each letter from red and plain dough. Place red letters in plain blocks and plain letters in red blocks; press lightly.

5. Bake 8 to 10 minutes. (Do not brown.) Cool on cookie sheets 1 minute. Remove to wire rack; cool completely.

Makes 2 dozen cookies

Note: The size of these cookies is determined by the size of the cookie cutters used. If smaller cookies are desired, use smaller cookie cutters and adjust the size of the dough log accordingly.

continued on page 22

abc blocks

christmas ornament cookie dough

2¼ **cups all-purpose flour**
¼ **teaspoon salt**
1 **cup sugar**
¾ **cup (1½ sticks) unsalted butter, softened**
1 **egg**
1 **teaspoon vanilla**
1 **teaspoon almond extract**

1. Combine flour and salt in medium bowl. Beat sugar and butter in large bowl at medium speed of electric mixer until fluffy.

2. Beat in egg, vanilla and almond extract. Gradually add flour mixture. Beat at low speed until well blended.

skippy quick cookies

1 **cup SKIPPY® Creamy or Super Chunk Peanut Butter**
1 **cup sugar**
1 **egg, slightly beaten**
1 **teaspoon vanilla extract**

Preheat oven to 325°F. In medium bowl, combine all ingredients. Shape dough into 1-inch balls. On ungreased baking sheets, arrange cookies 2 inches apart. With fork, gently flatten each cookie and press crisscross pattern into top.

Bake 8 minutes or until lightly browned and slightly puffed. Immediately top, if desired, with sprinkles, chocolate chips or chocolate candies. On wire rack, cool completely before removing from baking sheets.

Makes 2 dozen cookies

chocolate berry squares

 1 cup (2 sticks) butter or margarine, softened
 $\frac{1}{2}$ cup granulated sugar
 $\frac{1}{2}$ cup firmly packed light brown sugar
 1 large egg
 1 teaspoon vanilla extract
 2 cups all-purpose flour
 $\frac{3}{4}$ teaspoon baking soda
 $\frac{3}{4}$ teaspoon salt
 1$\frac{3}{4}$ cups "M&M's"® Semi-Sweet Chocolate Mini Baking Bits
 $\frac{1}{2}$ cup seedless red raspberry jam

Preheat oven to 350°F. Line 13×9×2-inch baking pan with aluminum foil, extending it 1 inch beyond each end of pan; set aside. In large bowl cream butter and sugars until light and fluffy; beat in egg and vanilla. In medium bowl combine flour, baking soda and salt; blend into creamed mixture. Stir in "M&M's"® Semi-Sweet Chocolate Mini Baking Bits. Reserve 1 cup dough. Spread remaining dough into prepared pan. Spread jam evenly over top of dough to within $\frac{1}{2}$ inch of edges. Drop reserved dough by teaspoonfuls randomly over jam. Bake 30 to 35 minutes or until light golden brown. Cool completely in pan. Remove by lifting foil. Cut into squares. Store in tightly covered container.

Makes 24 squares

cookie cups

1 package (20 ounces) refrigerated sugar cookie dough
All-purpose flour (optional)
Prepared pudding, nondairy whipped topping, maraschino cherries, jelly beans, assorted sprinkles and small candies

1. Grease 12 (2¾-inch) muffin cups.

2. Remove dough from wrapper according to package directions. Sprinkle dough with flour to minimize sticking, if necessary.

3. Cut dough into 12 equal pieces; roll into balls. Place 1 ball in bottom of each muffin cup. Press dough halfway up sides of muffin cups, making indentation in centers.

4. Freeze muffin cups 15 minutes. Preheat oven to 350°F.

5. Bake 15 to 17 minutes or until golden brown. Cookies will be puffy. Remove from oven; gently press indentations with teaspoon.

6. Return to oven 1 to 2 minutes. Cool cookies in muffin cups 5 minutes. Remove to wire rack; cool completely.

7. Fill each cookie cup with desired fillings. Decorate as desired.   *Makes 12 cookies*

Giant Cookie Cups Variation: Grease 10 (3¾-inch) muffin cups. Cut dough into 10 pieces; roll into balls. Complete recipe according to regular Cookie Cups directions. Makes 10 giant cookie cups.

Tip: Add some pizzazz to your cookie cups by filling with a mixture of prepared fruit-flavored gelatin combined with prepared pudding or nondairy whipped topping. For convenience, snack-size gelatins and puddings can be found at the supermarket, so there is no need to make them from scratch.

cookie cups

fruit and oat squares

1 cup all-purpose flour
1 cup uncooked quick oats
¾ cup packed light brown sugar
½ teaspoon baking soda
¼ teaspoon salt
¼ teaspoon ground cinnamon
⅓ cup butter or margarine, melted
¾ cup apricot, cherry or other fruit flavor preserves

1. Preheat oven to 350°F. Spray 9-inch square baking pan with nonstick cooking spray; set aside.

2. Combine flour, oats, brown sugar, baking soda, salt and cinnamon in medium bowl; mix well. Add butter; stir with fork until mixture is crumbly. Reserve ¾ cup crumb mixture for topping. Press remaining crumb mixture evenly onto bottom of prepared pan. Bake 5 to 7 minutes or until lightly browned. Spread preserves onto crust; sprinkle with reserved crumb mixture.

3. Bake 20 to 25 minutes or until golden brown. Cool completely in pan on wire rack. Cut into 16 squares.

Makes 16 servings

Tip: Store individually wrapped Fruit and Oat Squares at room temperature up to 3 days or freeze up to 1 month.

fruit and oat squares

banana chocolate cupcakes

    2 cups all-purpose flour
    ¾ cup sugar, divided
    ¼ cup unsweetened cocoa powder
    ¾ teaspoon baking soda
    ½ teaspoon baking powder
    ¼ teaspoon salt
    8 ounces low-fat plain or banana-flavored yogurt
    ½ cup mashed ripe banana (1 medium banana)
    ⅓ cup canola or vegetable oil
    ¼ cup fat-free (skim) milk
    2 teaspoons vanilla
    3 egg whites
       Powdered Sugar Glaze (recipe follows)

1. Preheat oven to 350°F. Line 20 (2½-inch) muffin cups with foil baking cups.

2. Combine flour, ¼ cup sugar, cocoa, baking soda, baking powder and salt in large bowl; set aside. Blend yogurt, banana, oil, milk and vanilla in small bowl; mix well.

3. Beat egg whites at medium speed with electric mixer until foamy. Gradually add remaining ½ cup sugar, beating well after each addition, until sugar is dissolved and stiff peaks form. Stir yogurt mixture into flour mixture just until dry ingredients are moistened. Gently fold in ⅓ of egg white mixture until blended; fold in remaining egg white mixture. Fill muffin cups ⅔ full with batter.

4. Bake 20 to 25 minutes or until toothpick inserted into centers comes out clean. Transfer cupcakes from pans to wire racks; cool completely. Drizzle Powdered Sugar Glaze over cupcakes; let stand until set. Store in airtight container at room temperature.

Makes 20 cupcakes

Powdered Sugar Glaze: Blend ½ cup powdered sugar and 1 tablespoon water in small bowl until smooth; add additional water, if necessary, to reach desired consistency.

banana chocolate
cupcakes

smiley oatmeal cookies

COOKIES
- 1 Butter Flavor CRISCO® Stick or 1 cup Butter Flavor CRISCO® all-vegetable shortening
- 1 cup firmly packed light brown sugar
- ¾ cup granulated sugar
- 2 eggs
- 1 teaspoon vanilla
- 2½ cups all-purpose flour
- 1 teaspoon baking soda
- ½ teaspoon salt
- 1 cup oats (quick or old-fashioned, uncooked)
- 1 cup flake coconut

FROSTING
- 2 cups confectioners' sugar
- ¼ Butter Flavor CRISCO® Stick or ¼ cup Butter Flavor CRISCO® all-vegetable shortening
- 5 to 6 teaspoons milk

DECORATION
- Peanut butter candy pieces
- Red licorice laces

1. Heat oven to 350°F. Place sheets of foil on countertop for cooling cookies.

2. For cookies, combine 1 cup shortening, brown sugar, granulated sugar, eggs and vanilla in large bowl. Beat at medium speed of electric mixer until well blended.

3. Combine flour, baking soda and salt. Add gradually to creamed mixture at low speed. Beat until well blended. Stir in oats and coconut with spoon. Shape tablespoonfuls of dough into 1-inch balls. Place 2 inches apart on ungreased baking sheet.

4. Bake at 350°F for 8 to 10 minutes or until very light brown and set. *Do not overbake.* Flatten slightly with spatula to level tops. Cool 2 minutes on baking sheet. Remove cookies to foil to cool completely.

5. For frosting, combine confectioners' sugar, ¼ cup shortening and milk in medium bowl. Beat at low speed until well blended and creamy. Spread thin layer on cookies. Decorate before frosting sets.

6. For decoration, make faces on cookies by placing candy pieces for eyes. Cut licorice into short strips. Form into different shapes for mouths. Press into frosting.

Makes about 5 dozen cookies

quick no-bake brownies

1 cup finely chopped nuts, divided
2 (1-ounce) squares unsweetened chocolate
1 (14-ounce) can EAGLE BRAND® Sweetened Condensed Milk (NOT evaporated milk)
2 to 2½ cups vanilla wafer crumbs (about 48 to 60 wafers)

1. Grease 9-inch square pan with butter. Sprinkle ¼ cup nuts evenly over bottom of pan. In heavy saucepan over low heat, melt chocolate with Eagle Brand. Cook and stir until mixture thickens, about 10 minutes.

2. Remove from heat; stir in crumbs and ½ cup nuts. Spread evenly in prepared pan.

3. Top with remaining ¼ cup nuts. Chill 4 hours or until firm. Cut into squares. Store loosely covered at room temperature.

Makes 24 brownies

Prep Time: 15 minutes • Chill Time: 4 hours

Wacky Snacky

goofy gus

  1 package (18 ounces) refrigerated sugar cookie dough
  1 egg yolk
  ¼ teaspoon water
  Red food coloring
  Prepared white frosting
 10 packages (2 cakes each) coconut and marshmallow covered, snowball-shaped cakes
  Assorted candies and tinted shredded coconut

1. Preheat oven to 350°F. Remove dough from wrapper; place in bowl. Let dough stand at room temperature about 15 minutes.

2. Roll dough to ⅛-inch thickness on well-floured surface. Cut with 2¼-inch foot-shaped cookie cutter. Place cutouts 2 inches apart on ungreased cookie sheets, flipping half of cookies over to make both left and right feet.

3. Combine egg yolk, water and food coloring in small bowl; stir until well blended. Using small, clean craft paintbrush, paint egg yolk mixture on feet to make toenails.

4. Bake 5 to 8 minutes or until golden brown. Remove to wire racks; cool completely.

5. Using small amount of frosting, attach 1 right and 1 left foot to each snowball cake. Decorate with assorted candies and coconut as desired. *Makes 20 desserts*

goofy gus

s'mores on a stick

1 (14-ounce) can EAGLE BRAND® Sweetened Condensed Milk (NOT evaporated milk), divided
1½ cups milk chocolate mini chips, divided
1 cup miniature marshmallows
11 whole graham crackers, halved crosswise
Toppings: chopped peanuts, mini candy-coated chocolate pieces, sprinkles

1. Microwave half of Eagle Brand in microwave-safe bowl at HIGH (100% power) 1½ minutes. Stir in 1 cup chips until smooth; stir in marshmallows.

2. Spread chocolate mixture evenly by heaping tablespoonfuls onto 11 graham cracker halves. Top with remaining graham cracker halves; place on waxed paper.

3. Microwave remaining Eagle Brand at HIGH (100% power) 1½ minutes; stir in remaining ½ cup chips, stirring until smooth. Drizzle mixture over cookies and sprinkle with desired toppings.

4. Let stand for 2 hours; insert a wooden craft stick into center of each cookie.

Makes 11 servings

Prep Time: 10 minutes • Cook Time: 3 minutes

35

s'mores on a stick

puzzle cookie

¾ **cup shortening**
½ **cup packed light brown sugar**
6 **tablespoons dark molasses**
2 **egg whites**
¾ **teaspoon vanilla**
2¼ **cups all-purpose flour**
2 **teaspoons ground cinnamon**
¾ **teaspoon baking soda**
¾ **teaspoon salt**
¾ **teaspoon ground ginger**
¼ **teaspoon plus** ⅛ **teaspoon baking powder**
Assorted colored frostings, colored sugars, colored decorator gels and small candies

1. Beat shortening, brown sugar, molasses, egg whites and vanilla in large bowl at high speed of electric mixer until smooth.

2. Combine flour, cinnamon, baking soda, salt, ginger and baking powder in medium bowl. Add to shortening mixture; mix well. Shape dough into flat rectangle. Wrap in plastic wrap and refrigerate about 8 hours or until firm.

3. Preheat oven to 350°F. Grease 15½×10½-inch jelly-roll pan.

4. Sprinkle dough with additional flour. Roll out to 15×10-inch rectangle. Transfer to prepared pan. Cut shapes into dough using cookie cutters or free-hand, using sharp knife, allowing at least 1 inch between each shape. Cut through dough, but do not remove shapes.

5. Bake 12 minutes or until edges begin to brown lightly. Remove from oven and retrace shapes with knife. Return to oven 5 to 6 minutes. Cool in pan 5 minutes. Carefully remove shapes to wire racks; cool completely.

continued on page 38

puzzle cookie

puzzle cookie, continued

6. Decorate shapes with frostings, sugars, decorator gels and small candies. Leave puzzle frame in pan. Decorate with frostings, colored sugars and gels. Return shapes to their respective openings to complete puzzle.   *Makes 1 cookie puzzle*

dirt bites

4½ cups party mix or crispy multigrain cereal
 2 tablespoons Butter Flavor CRISCO® Shortening or Butter Flavor CRISCO® Stick
½ cup chocolate chips
¼ cup peanut butter
½ teaspoon vanilla
¾ cup powdered sugar

Measure party mix or cereal and set aside in large mixing bowl.

Melt CRISCO® shortening, chocolate chips and peanut butter together in saucepan on low heat (or microwave on 50% power checking at 1 minute intervals).

Remove mixture from heat and stir in vanilla.

Pour over cereal and mix until all coated.

Add powdered sugar to zipper bag; add coated cereal and toss to coat all.

Spread double coated cereal onto sheet of wax paper to cool. Pick up coated cereal with hands and store in clean zipper bag. Discard excess sugar. Refrigerate.   *Makes 4½ cups*

magic wands

INGREDIENTS
   1 cup semisweet chocolate chips
   12 pretzel rods
   3 ounces white chocolate baking bars or confectionery coating
      Red and yellow food colorings
      Assorted sprinkles

SUPPLIES
   Ribbon

1. Line baking sheet with waxed paper.

2. Melt semisweet chocolate in top of double boiler over hot, not boiling, water. Remove from heat. Dip pretzel rods into chocolate, spooning chocolate to coat about ³/₄ of each pretzel. Place on prepared baking sheet. Refrigerate until chocolate is firm.

3. Melt white chocolate in top of clean double boiler over hot, not boiling, water. Stir in food colorings to make orange. Remove from heat. Dip coated pretzels quickly into colored white chocolate to coat about ¹/₄ of each pretzel.

4. Place on baking sheet. Immediately top with sprinkles. Refrigerate until chocolate is firm.

5. Tie ends with ribbons.

Makes 12 wands

Hershey's easy chocolate cracker snacks

1²/₃ cups (10-ounce package) HERSHEY'S Mint Chocolate Chips*
2 cups (12-ounce package) HERSHEY'S Semi-Sweet Chocolate Chips
2 tablespoons shortening (do not use butter, margarine, spread or oil)
60 to 70 round buttery crackers (about one-half 1-pound box)

*2 cups (11.5-ounce package) HERSHEY'S Milk Chocolate Chips and ¼ teaspoon pure peppermint extract can be substituted for mint chocolate chips.

1. Line several trays or cookie sheets with waxed paper.

2. Place mint chocolate chips, chocolate chips and shortening in large microwave-safe bowl. Microwave at HIGH (100%) 1 minute; stir. Continue heating 30 seconds at a time, stirring after each heating, until chips are melted and mixture is smooth when stirred.

3. Drop crackers into chocolate mixture one at a time. Using tongs, push cracker into chocolate so that it is covered completely. (If chocolate begins to thicken, reheat 10 to 20 seconds in microwave.) Remove from chocolate, tapping lightly on edge of bowl to remove excess chocolate. Place on prepared tray. Refrigerate until chocolate hardens, about 20 minutes. For best results, store tightly covered in refrigerator.

Makes about 5½ dozen cookies

Peanut Butter and Milk Chocolate: Use 1²/₃ cups (10-ounce package) REESE'S® Peanut Butter Chips, 2 cups (11.5-ounce package) HERSHEY'S Milk Chocolate Chips and 2 tablespoons shortening. Proceed as above.

Chocolate Raspberry: Use 1²/₃ cups (10-ounce package) HERSHEY'S Raspberry Chips, 2 cups (11.5-ounce package) HERSHEY'S Milk Chocolate Chips and 2 tablespoons shortening. Proceed as above.

White Chip and Toffee: Melt 2 cups (12-ounce package) HERSHEY'S Premier White Chips and 1 tablespoon shortening. Before coating hardens sprinkle with SKOR® English Toffee Bits or HEATH® BITS 'O BRICKLE® Almond Toffee Bits.

Hershey's easy chocolate
cracker snacks

maraschino-lemonade pops

1 (10-ounce) jar maraschino cherries
8 (3-ounce) paper cups
1 (12-ounce) can frozen pink lemonade concentrate, partly thawed
¼ cup water
8 popsicle sticks

Drain cherries, reserving the juice. Put one whole cherry in each paper cup. Coarsely chop the remaining cherries. Put chopped cherries, lemonade concentrate, water and reserved juice in the container of an electric blender or food processor. Purée until smooth. Fill paper cups with equal amounts of cherry mixture. Freeze 30 to 40 minutes, or until very slushy. Place popsicle sticks in the center of each cup. Freeze 1 hour longer, or until firm. To serve, peel off paper cups. *Makes 8 servings*

Favorite recipe from **Cherry Marketing Institute**

polar bear banana bites

1 medium banana, cut into 6 equal-size pieces
¼ cup creamy peanut butter
3 tablespoons fat-free (skim) milk
¼ cup miniature-size marshmallows
2 tablespoons unsalted dry-roasted peanuts, chopped
1 tablespoon chocolate-flavored decorator sprinkles

1. Insert toothpick into each banana piece. Place on tray lined with waxed paper.

2. Whisk together peanut butter and milk. Combine marshmallows, peanuts and chocolate sprinkles in shallow dish. Dip each banana piece in peanut butter mixture, draining off excess. Roll in marshmallow mixture. Place on tray; let stand until set.

Makes 3 servings

pop corn s'mores

2 quarts popped JOLLY TIME® Pop Corn

15 graham cracker squares

4 cups miniature marshmallows, divided

1 cup semi-sweet chocolate pieces

2 tablespoons butter or margarine

Preheat oven to 350°F. Put popped pop corn in large bowl. Arrange graham cracker squares in bottom of 13×9-inch baking pan; trim slightly if necessary to fit pan. Sprinkle with 2 cups marshmallows and chocolate pieces. Place butter in 2-quart glass measuring pitcher. Microwave at HIGH (100% power) until butter is melted, about 45 seconds. Stir in remaining 2 cups marshmallows until well coated. Microwave at HIGH (100% power) until marshmallows look puffy, about 1 minute; stir to melt completely. Pour marshmallow mixture over popped pop corn and mix well. Spread coated pop corn evenly over chocolate pieces in pan. Bake until marshmallows are puffy and appear to be melted, about 6 minutes. Invert pan onto cutting board and cut into squares between graham crackers.

Makes 15 s'mores

ho ho® pudding

1 box of HO HO'S®

2 packages chocolate pudding mix

4 cups milk

1 large tub whipped topping

Cut Ho Ho's into circles, saving 1 Ho Ho. Mix pudding and milk according to package pudding directions and chill until thick. In large glass bowl, layer Ho Ho's, pudding and whipped topping. Ending with whipped topping. Take remaining Ho Ho and slice in circles and place on top. Keep refrigerated until ready to eat.

Makes 4 servings

green meanies

4 green apples
1 cup nut butter (cashew, almond or peanut butter)
Almond slivers

1. Place apple, stem side up, on cutting board. Cut away 2 halves from sides of apple, leaving a 1-inch-thick center slice with stem and core. Discard core slice. Cut each half round into 4 wedges using crinkle cutter. Repeat with remaining apples. Each apple will yield 8 wedges.

2. Spread 2 teaspoons nut butter on wide edge of apple slice. Top with another crinkled edge apple slice, aligning crinkled edges to resemble jaws. Insert almond slivers to make fangs. *Makes 8 servings*

Tip: For best effect, use a crinkle cutter garnishing tool to create a toothy look.

double peanut snack mix

4 cups sweet shredded oat cereal
1 cup peanuts
½ cup butter or margarine
½ cup JIF® Creamy Peanut Butter
1 teaspoon ground cinnamon

Preheat oven to 350°F.

In large bowl, combine cereal and peanuts.

In small saucepan, heat butter or margarine, JIF® peanut butter and cinnamon over low heat until butter and JIF® are melted. Stir until blended.

Slowly pour over cereal mixture, mixing well.

Spread into 13×9×2-inch baking pan.

Bake 10 to 12 minutes; stir occasionally. Cool. *Makes 4 cups*

green meanies

potato bugs

1 package (16 ounces) shredded potato nuggets
6 pieces uncooked spaghetti, broken into thirds
1 carrot, cut into 1½-inch strips
    Sour cream, black olive slices, ketchup and broccoli pieces

- Preheat oven to 450°F. Lightly grease baking sheets.

- Spread potato nuggets on baking sheets. Bake 7 minutes. Loosen nuggets from baking sheets with metal spatula.

- Thread 3 potato nuggets onto 1 spaghetti piece. Bake 5 minutes.

- Carefully push carrot strips into sides of each nugget for legs. Using sour cream to attach vegetables, decorate faces as shown in photo. *Makes about 15 servings*

Tip Let the kids to help you assemble these cute crawlers and decorate them as they like.

47

top to bottom: grilled cheese
jack-o'-lanterns (page 74)
and potato bugs

monster pops

1 2/3 cups all-purpose flour
1 teaspoon baking soda
1/2 teaspoon salt
1 cup (2 sticks) butter or margarine, softened
3/4 cup granulated sugar
3/4 cup packed brown sugar
2 teaspoons vanilla extract
2 large eggs
2 cups (12-ounce package) NESTLÉ® TOLL HOUSE® Semi-Sweet Chocolate Morsels
2 cups quick or old-fashioned oats
1 cup raisins
About 24 wooden craft sticks
1 container (16 ounces) prepared vanilla frosting, colored as desired, or colored icing in tubes
Colored candies (such as WONKA® RUNTS and/or NERDS)

PREHEAT oven to 325°F.

COMBINE flour, baking soda and salt in small bowl. Beat butter, granulated sugar, brown sugar and vanilla extract in large mixer bowl until creamy. Beat in eggs. Gradually beat in flour mixture. Stir in morsels, oats and raisins. Drop dough by level 1/4-cup measure 3 inches apart onto ungreased baking sheets. Shape into round mounds. Insert wooden stick into side of each mound.

BAKE for 14 to 18 minutes or until golden brown. Cool on baking sheets on wire racks for 2 minutes; remove to wire racks to cool completely. **DECORATE** pops as desired.

Makes about 2 dozen cookies

For Speedy Monster Pops: **SUBSTITUTE** 2 packages (18 ounce each), NESTLÉ® TOLL HOUSE® Refrigerated Chocolate Chip Cookie Dough for the first nine ingredients, adding 1 cup quick or old-fashioned oats and 1/2 cup raisins to the dough. Bake as stated above for 16 to 20 minutes or until golden brown. Makes 1 1/2 dozen cookies.

monster pops

stuffed banana smiles

1 medium size banana, with peel on
1 tablespoon SUN-MAID® Raisins or Golden Raisins
1 tablespoon semi-sweet, milk or white chocolate baking chips

1. **PLACE** banana, with peel on, flat on its side on a microwave-safe plate.

2. **STARTING*** and ending ¼-inch from the ends of banana, cut a slit lengthwise through the banana up to the skin on the other side.

3. **GENTLY** open the banana. Use your fingers to stuff the banana with raisins, then add chocolate chips.

4. **MICROWAVE*** banana uncovered on HIGH for 40 to 60 seconds or until chocolate begins to melt and banana is still firm. Banana skin may darken slightly. Eat immediately, scooping with a spoon right out of the banana peel. *Makes 1 serving*

*Adult Supervision Suggested

Tip: At a party, invite guests to prepare their own banana smile!

Tip: On your grill,* place each banana flat on its side, on a piece of aluminum foil and follow steps 2 and 3 above. Wrap bananas loosely and pinch foil closed. Place on covered grill or over hot coals for about 5 minutes or just until chocolate begins to melt and banana is still firm.

Prep Time: 2 minutes • Bake Time: 1 minute

crisp tortellini bites

½ **cup plain dry bread crumbs**

2 **teaspoons HERB-OX® chicken flavored bouillon granules**

¼ **teaspoon garlic powder**

¼ **cup grated Parmesan cheese**

½ **cup sour cream**

2 **tablespoons milk**

1 **(9-ounce) package refrigerated cheese filled tortellini**

   Warm pizza sauce or marinara sauce, for dipping

Heat oven to 400°F. In bowl, combine bread crumbs, bouillon, garlic powder and Parmesan cheese. In another small bowl, combine sour cream and milk. Dip tortellini in sour cream mixture, then in the bread crumbs; coat evenly. Place tortellini on baking sheet. Bake 10 to 12 minutes, or until crisp and golden brown; turning once. Serve immediately with warm pizza or marinara sauce. *Makes 8 servings*

Prep Time: 15 minutes • Total Time: 30 minutes

Tip The bouillon mixture makes a great coating for chicken fingers or mild fish.

peanut butter aliens

   1 package (18 ounces) refrigerated sugar cookie dough
   ½ cup creamy peanut butter
   ⅓ cup all-purpose flour
   ¼ cup powdered sugar
   ½ teaspoon vanilla
   1 cup strawberry jam
     Green decorating icing

1. Preheat oven to 350°F. Grease 2 cookie sheets. Remove dough from wrapper; place in large bowl. Let dough stand at room temperature about 15 minutes.

2. Add peanut butter, flour, powdered sugar and vanilla to dough; beat at medium speed of electric mixer until well blended. Divide dough in half; wrap 1 half in plastic wrap and refrigerate.

3. Roll remaining dough to ¼-inch thickness on lightly floured surface. Cut into 14 (3-inch) rounds; pinch 1 side of each circle to make tear drop shape. Place cutouts 2 inches apart on prepared cookie sheets. Bake 12 to 14 minutes or until firm and lightly browned. Cool on cookie sheets 2 to 3 minutes. Remove to wire rack; cool completely.

4. Roll remaining dough to ¼-inch thickness on lightly floured surface. Cut into 14 (3-inch) rounds; pinch 1 side of each circle to make tear drop shape. Place cutouts 2 inches apart on prepared cookie sheets. Using sharp knife or mini cookie cutter, cut 2 oblong holes for eyes. Make small slit or third hole for mouth, if desired. Bake 12 to 14 minutes or until firm and lightly browned. Cool on cookie sheets 2 to 3 minutes. Remove to wire rack; cool completely.

5. Spread green icing on cookies with faces; let stand 10 minutes or until set. Spread about 1 tablespoon jam on each uncut cookie. To assemble, cover each jam-topped cookie with green face cookie.

Makes 14 sandwich cookies

peanut butter aliens

witches' snack hats

1 package (18 ounces) refrigerated sugar cookie dough
¼ cup unsweetened cocoa powder
1½ cups semisweet chocolate chips, divided
16 sugar ice cream cones
⅓ cup butter
3 cups dry cereal (mixture of puffed corn, bite-size wheat and toasted oat cereal)
½ cup roasted pumpkin seeds
½ cup chopped dried cherries or raisins
1⅓ cups powdered sugar
Assorted colored sugars and decors

1. Preheat oven to 350°F. Grease cookie sheets; set aside. Remove dough from wrapper according to package directions. Combine dough and cocoa powder in large bowl; mix until well blended. Evenly divide dough into 16 pieces; shape into balls. Flatten each ball onto prepared cookie sheet into 3½- to 4-inch circle. Bake 6 to 8 minutes or until set. Cool on cookie sheets 5 minutes; transfer to wire racks to cool completely.

2. Line large tray with waxed paper. Place 1 cup chocolate chips in small microwavable bowl. Microwave at HIGH 1 to 1½ minutes or until melted, stirring at 30-second intervals. Coat outside of sugar cones with chocolate using clean pastry brush. Stand up on prepared tray; let set.

3. Place remaining ½ cup chocolate chips and butter in small microwavable bowl. Microwave at HIGH 1 to 1½ minutes or until melted, stirring at 30-second intervals. Stir mixture to blend well. Place cereal, pumpkin seeds and cherries in large bowl. Pour chocolate mixture over cereal mixture and stir until thoroughly coated. Sprinkle mixture with powdered sugar, ⅓ cup at a time, carefully folding and mixing until thoroughly coated.

4. Fill cone with snack mix. Brush cone edge with melted chocolate; attach to center of cookie and let set. Repeat with remaining cones, snack mix and cookies. Decorate hats as desired with melted chocolate, colored sugars and decors. *Makes 16 servings*

Hint: To use these hats as place cards, simply write each guest's name on the hat with melted white chocolate, frosting or decorating gel.

teddy bear party mix

4 cups crisp cinnamon graham cereal
2 cups honey flavored teddy-shaped graham snacks
1 can (1½ ounces) *French's* Potato Sticks
3 tablespoons melted unsalted butter
2 tablespoons *French's* Worcestershire Sauce
1 tablespoon packed brown sugar
¼ teaspoon ground cinnamon
1 cup sweetened dried cranberries or raisins
½ cup chocolate, peanut butter or carob chips

1. Preheat oven to 350°F. Lightly spray jelly-roll pan with nonstick cooking spray. Combine cereal, graham snacks and potato sticks in large bowl.

2. Combine butter, Worcestershire, sugar and cinnamon in small bowl; toss with cereal mixture. Transfer to prepared pan. Bake 12 minutes. Cool completely.

3. Stir in dried cranberries and chips. Store in an air-tight container.

Makes about 7 cups

Prep Time: 5 minutes • Cook Time: 12 minutes

sugar cookie fruit tartlets

1 package (18 ounces) refrigerated sugar cookie dough
1 package (8 ounces) fat-free cream cheese, softened
¼ cup orange marmalade
1 teaspoon vanilla
1 packet sugar substitute *or* equivalent of 2 teaspoons sugar
  Assorted fresh and/or canned fruit

1. Preheat oven to 375°F. Lightly grease cookie sheets.

2. Remove dough from wrapper, keeping in log shape. Cut dough into 16 slices. Arrange cookie slices 2 inches apart on prepared cookie sheets. Bake 10 to 14 minutes or until edges are lightly browned. Cool on cookie sheets 1 minute. Remove to wire rack; cool completely.

3. Meanwhile for frosting, beat cream cheese, marmalade, vanilla and sugar substitute in medium bowl at high speed of electric mixer until well blended. Cover with plastic wrap; refrigerate until ready to use.

4. Spread frosting on cooled cookies. Arrange fruit on top of frosting to create butterflies, flowers or other designs as desired. Serve immediately or store in tightly covered container in refrigerator.

Makes 16 servings

sugar cookie fruit tartlets

peanut butter fruit dip

2 cups skim milk
½ cup light sour cream
1 (3.4-ounce) package vanilla instant pudding and pie filling mix
1 cup JIF® Reduced Fat Peanut Butter
⅓ cup sugar
Apple and banana slices (or any fruit of your choice)

Combine milk, sour cream and pudding mix in medium bowl. Whisk until smooth. Stir JIF® peanut butter until evenly mixed throughout; measure after stirring. Stir peanut butter and sugar into pudding mixture; mix until well blended.

Serve with sliced apples or banana chunks. Store in refrigerator. If dip becomes too thick, stir in additional milk.

Makes 3 cups

Variation: Try stirring in ¼ cup SMUCKER'S® Hot Fudge Ice Cream Topping to make a rich peanut butter and chocolate dessert dip.

cosmic cups

1½ cups boiling water
2 packages (4-serving size) or 1 package (8-serving size) Berry Blue or lime flavor gelatin
¾ cup cold water
Ice cubes
1 can (15.25 ounces) DOLE® Pineapple Cosmic Fun Shapes®, drained

• Stir boiling water into gelatin in large bowl at least 2 minutes until completely dissolved. Mix cold water and ice to make 2 cups. Add to gelatin, stirring until slightly thickened. If necessary, refrigerate to thicken gelatin. Stir in pineapple fun shapes. Divide among 10 dessert dishes or spoon into 2-quart bowl.

• Refrigerate 3 hours or until firm.

Makes 10 servings

Contents

Loony Lunches

silly snake sandwich

½ cup peanut butter

1 loaf (½ pound) sliced French or Italian bread, about 11 inches long and 3 inches wide

½ cup jelly, any flavor

1 red bell pepper

1 each black olive and green olive

¼ cup marshmallow creme

1. Using small amount of peanut butter, attach first 2 inches (3 to 4 slices) bread loaf together to make snake head. Cut bell pepper into 2-inch-long tongue shape. Make very small horizontal slice in heel of bread, being careful not to cut all the way through. Place "tongue" into slice. Cut black olive in half lengthwise; attach with peanut butter to snake head for eyes. Cut 2 small pieces from green olive; attach with peanut butter for nostrils. Set snake head aside.

2. Combine remaining peanut butter, jelly and marshmallow creme in small bowl until smooth. Spread on half of bread slices; top with remaining bread slices.

3. Place snake head on large serving tray. Arrange sandwiches in wavy pattern to resemble slithering snake. Serve immediately.   *Makes about 8 small sandwiches*

silly snake sandwich

monster finger sandwiches

　　1 can (11 ounces) refrigerated breadstick dough (12 breadsticks)
　　　Mustard
　12 slices deli ham, cut into ½-inch strips
　　4 slices Monterey Jack cheese, cut into ½-inch strips
　　1 egg yolk, lightly beaten
　　　Assorted food colorings

1. Preheat oven to 350°F. Place 6 breadsticks on ungreased baking sheets. Spread with mustard as desired. Divide ham strips evenly among breadsticks, placing over mustard. Repeat with cheese. Top with remaining 6 breadsticks. Gently stretch top dough over filling; press doughs together to seal.

2. Score knuckle and nail lines into each sandwich using sharp knife. Do not cut completely through dough. Tint egg yolk with food coloring as desired. Paint nail with egg yolk mixture.

3. Bake on lower oven rack 12 to 13 minutes or just until light golden. Let cool slightly. Serve warm or cool completely. *Makes 6 servings*

monster finger sandwiches

dizzy dogs

1 package (8 breadsticks or 11 ounces) refrigerated breadsticks
1 package (16 ounces) hot dogs (8 hot dogs)
1 egg white
   Sesame and/or poppy seeds
   Mustard, ketchup and barbecue sauce (optional)

1. Preheat oven to 375°F.

2. Using 1 breadstick for each, wrap hot dogs with dough in spiral pattern. Brush breadstick dough with egg white and sprinkle with sesame and/or poppy seeds. Place on ungreased baking sheet.

3. Bake 12 to 15 minutes or until light golden brown. Serve with condiments for dipping, if desired. *Makes 8 hot dogs*

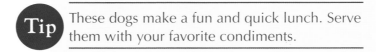

Tip These dogs make a fun and quick lunch. Serve them with your favorite condiments.

candy corn by the slice

1 package (10 ounces) refrigerated pizza crust dough
2 cups (8 ounces) shredded Cheddar cheese, divided
2 tablespoons paprika
¼ cup white cheese sauce*
½ cup shredded mozzarella cheese
⅓ cup tomato sauce

To make a white cheese sauce, mix 3 tablespoons vegetable broth with 3 tablespoons mascarpone cheese in a small saucepan over low heat, until melted. Season with salt and white pepper to taste.

1. Preheat oven to 400°F. Spray a 13-inch round pizza pan with cooking spray. Fit pizza dough into pan, shaping as needed.

2. Place 1 cup Cheddar cheese in a medium bowl. Add paprika and stir until cheese is evenly colored; set aside. Make white cheese sauce.

3. Spread white cheese sauce in center of pizza in a 4-inch diameter circle. Arrange mozzarella cheese on top of white sauce. Place a 3-inch ring of tomato sauce around center circle; top with red-colored Cheddar cheese. Use remaining 1 cup Cheddar cheese to create a 1½-inch border around edge of pizza.

4. Bake 12 to 15 minutes or until edge is lightly browned and cheese is melted and bubbling. Cut into wedges to serve. *Makes 8 slices*

candy corn by the slice

barbecue flying saucers with vegetable martians

½ teaspoon black pepper*
1 (10-ounce) pork tenderloin*
¼ cup barbecue sauce
½ teaspoon prepared mustard
1 (7½-ounce) package (10) refrigerated buttermilk biscuits
1 egg yolk (optional)
1 teaspoon water (optional)
3 to 4 drops food coloring (optional)
   Vegetable Martians (page 70)

*Substitute 10 ounces lean deli roasted pork for pork tenderloin and pepper, if desired.

1. Preheat oven to 425°F. Rub pepper on outside of pork tenderloin. Place pork in shallow roasting pan. Roast 15 to 25 minutes or until meat thermometer inserted into thickest part of meat registers 160°F. Remove from oven; let stand 5 minutes. Shred pork.

2. Reduce oven temperature to 400°F. Stir together barbecue sauce and mustard. Toss with shredded pork.

3. Roll each biscuit on lightly floured surface into 4-inch circle. Place one fifth of pork mixture on each of five circles. Moisten edges. Top with remaining biscuit circles. Crimp edges to seal.

4. Stir together egg yolk, water and food coloring to make egg-wash paint, if desired. Using clean paintbrush, paint desired designs on biscuit "flying saucers." Place on baking sheet. Bake 11 to 13 minutes or until golden.   *Makes 5 servings*

continued on page 70

69

barbecue flying saucer with
vegetable martian

barbecue flying saucers with vegetable martians, continued

vegetable martians

10 cherry tomatoes, baby pattypan squash or combination
5 to 10 thin slices cucumber or zucchini
¼ teaspoon reduced-fat soft cream cheese or mustard
5 to 8 currants or raisins, cut into halves
10 chow mein noodles

Skewer vegetables on toothpicks to form martian bodies. Use cream cheese or mustard to make eyes or to attach currants for eyes and mouths. Press 2 chow mein noodles into top of each martian for antennae. Remove toothpicks before serving.   *Makes 5 martians*

tuna schooners

2 (3-ounce) cans water-packed light tuna, drained
½ cup finely chopped apple
¼ cup shredded carrot
⅓ cup reduced-fat ranch salad dressing
2 English muffins, split and lightly toasted
8 triangular-shaped baked whole wheat crackers or triangular-shaped tortilla chips

1. Combine tuna, apple and carrot in medium bowl. Add salad dressing; stir to combine.

2. Spread ¼ of tuna mixture over top of each muffin half. Stand 2 crackers and press firmly into tuna mixture on each muffin half to form 'sails.'   *Makes 4 servings*

cheesy chicken tortillas

4 boneless, skinless chicken breast halves (about 1½ pounds)
2 tablespoons CRISCO® Oil*
1 can (10 ounces) mild green chili enchilada sauce**
2 cans (4 ounces each) diced green chilies
8 (10-inch) flour tortillas
1 package (8 ounces) shredded Cheddar cheese (2 cups)
   Shredded lettuce
   Chopped tomatoes
   Sour cream
   Guacamole

*Use your favorite Crisco Oil product.

**Substitute red enchilada sauce if green is unavailable.

1. Heat oven to 350°F.

2. Rinse chicken; pat dry. Cut into bite-size pieces. Stir-fry in oil until no longer pink. Stir in enchilada sauce and chilies. Simmer about 4 minutes.

3. Oil 2 jelly-roll or other large flat pans. Place 2 tortillas on each pan. Bake at 350°F for 8 minutes or until slightly golden. *Do not overbake.*

4. Remove pans from oven. Spoon chicken mixture evenly over baked tortillas. Top each with cheese. Cover with remaining unheated tortillas.

5. Return pans to oven for 10 minutes or until top tortillas are slightly golden. *Do not overbake.* Remove from oven. Cut into quarters. Top with lettuce, tomatoes, sour cream and guacamole.

Makes 4 to 5 servings

sloppy goblins

1 pound 90% lean ground beef

1 cup chopped onion

5 hot dogs, cut into ½-inch pieces

½ cup ketchup

¼ cup chopped dill pickle

¼ cup honey

¼ cup tomato paste

¼ cup prepared mustard

2 teaspoons cider vinegar

1 teaspoon Worcestershire sauce

8 hamburger buns

  Green olives, ripe olives, banana pepper slices, carrot curls and crinkles, red pepper, parsley sprigs and pretzel sticks

1. Cook beef and onion in large skillet over medium heat until beef is brown and onion is tender; drain. Stir in remaining ingredients except buns and decorations. Cook, covered, 5 minutes or until heated through.

2. Spoon meat mixture onto bottoms of buns; cover with tops of buns. Serve with decorations and let each person create a goblin face. Refrigerate leftovers.

Makes 8 servings

funny face sandwich melts

2 super-size English muffins, split and toasted
8 teaspoons *French's*® Sweet & Tangy Honey Mustard
1 can (8 ounces) crushed pineapple, drained
8 ounces sliced smoked ham
4 slices Swiss cheese or white American cheese

1. Place English muffins, cut side up, on baking sheet. Spread each with *2 teaspoons* mustard. Arrange one-fourth of the pineapple, ham and cheese on top, dividing evenly.

2. Broil until cheese melts, about 1 minute. Decorate with mustard and assorted vegetables to create your own funny face.   *Makes 4 servings*

Tip: This sandwich is also easy to prepare in the toaster oven.

Prep Time: 10 minutes • Cook Time: 1 minute

grilled cheese jack-o'-lanterns

3 tablespoons butter or margarine, softened
8 slices bread
4 slices Monterey Jack cheese
4 slices sharp Cheddar cheese

• Preheat oven to 350°F. Spread butter on one side of each bread slice. Place bread buttered-side-down on ungreased cookie sheet.

• Using small sharp knife, cut out shapes from 4 bread slices to make jack-o'-lantern faces. On remaining bread slices layer 1 slice Monterey Jack and 1 slice Cheddar.

• Bake 10 to 12 minutes or until cheese is melted. Remove from oven; place jack-o'-lantern bread slice on cheese sandwiches and serve.   *Makes 4 servings*

75
hawaiian funny face
sandwich melt

colorful kabobs

30 cocktail-size smoked sausages

10 to 20 cherry or grape tomatoes

10 to 20 large pimiento-stuffed green olives

 2 yellow bell peppers, cut into 1-inch squares

¼ cup butter or margarine, melted

Lemon juice (optional)

1. Preheat oven to 450°F.

2. Thread 3 sausages onto 8-inch wooden skewer*, alternating with tomatoes, olives and bell peppers. Repeat on remaining nine skewers.

3. Place skewers on rack in shallow baking pan. Brush with melted butter and drizzle with lemon juice, if desired. Bake 4 to 6 minutes until hot.   *Makes 10 kabobs*

Soak skewers in water 20 minutes before using to prevent them from burning.

Tip: For younger children, remove food from skewers and serve in a paper cup or bowl. It's still portable, but much safer.

colorful kabobs

super spread sandwich stars

1 Red or Golden Delicious apple, peeled, cored and coarsely chopped
1 cup roasted peanuts
$\frac{1}{3}$ cup honey
1 tablespoon lemon juice
1 teaspoon ground cinnamon
Sliced sandwich bread

For Super Spread, place chopped apple, peanuts, honey, lemon juice and cinnamon in food processor or blender. Pulse food processor several times until ingredients start to blend, occasionally scraping down the sides with rubber spatula. Process 1 to 2 minutes until mixture is smooth and spreadable.

For Sandwich Stars, use butter knife to spread about 1 tablespoon Super Spread on 2 slices of bread. Stack them together, spread side up. Top with third slice bread. Place star-shaped cookie cutter on top of sandwich; press down firmly and evenly. Leaving cookie cutter in place, remove excess trimmings with your fingers or a butter knife. Remove cookie cutter.

Makes 1¼ cups spread (enough for about 10 sandwiches)

Favorite recipe from **Texas Peanut Producers Board**

hot dog burritos

1 can (16 ounces) pork and beans
⅓ cup ketchup
2 tablespoons brown sugar
2 tablespoons *French's*® Classic Yellow® Mustard
8 frankfurters, cooked
8 (8-inch) flour tortillas, heated

1. Combine beans, ketchup, brown sugar and mustard in medium saucepan. Bring to boil over medium-high heat. Reduce heat to low and simmer 2 minutes.

2. Arrange frankfurters in heated tortillas and top with bean mixture. Roll up jelly-roll style.

Makes 8 servings

Prep Time: 5 minutes • Cook Time: 8 minutes

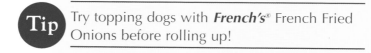

Tip Try topping dogs with *French's*® French Fried Onions before rolling up!

81

hot dog burrito

stuffed bundles

1 package (10 ounces) refrigerated pizza dough
2 ounces lean ham or turkey ham, chopped
½ cup (2 ounces) shredded reduced-fat sharp Cheddar cheese

1. Preheat oven to 425°F. Coat nonstick 12-cup muffin pan with nonstick cooking spray.

2. Unroll dough on flat surface; cut into 12 pieces (4×3-inch rectangles)

3. Divide ham and cheese between dough rectangles. Bring corners of dough together, pinching to seal. Place, smooth side up, in prepared muffin cups.

4. Bake 10 to 12 minutes or until golden.   *Makes 12 servings*

pizza soup

2 cans (10¾ ounces each) condensed tomato soup
¾ teaspoon garlic powder
½ teaspoon dried oregano leaves
¾ cup uncooked tiny pasta shells (¼-inch)
1 cup shredded quick-melting mozzarella cheese
1 cup *French's*® French Fried Onions

1. Combine soup, *2 soup cans of water,* garlic powder and oregano in small saucepan. Bring to boiling over medium-high heat.

2. Add pasta. Cook 8 minutes or until pasta is tender.

3. Stir in cheese. Cook until cheese melts. Sprinkle with French Fried Onions.

Makes 4 servings

Prep Time: 5 minutes • Cook Time: 10 minutes

pizza snack cups

1 can (12 ounces) refrigerated biscuits (10 biscuits)
½ pound ground beef
1 jar (14 ounces) RAGÚ® Pizza Quick® Sauce
½ cup shredded mozzarella cheese (about 2 ounces)

1. Preheat oven to 375°F. In muffin pan, evenly press each biscuit in bottom and up side of each cup; chill until ready to fill.

2. In 10-inch skillet, brown ground beef over medium-high heat; drain. Stir in Ragú Pizza Quick Sauce and heat through.

3. Evenly spoon beef mixture into prepared muffin cups. Bake 15 minutes. Sprinkle with cheese and bake an additional 5 minutes or until cheese is melted and biscuits are golden. Let stand 5 minutes. Gently remove pizza cups from muffin pan and serve.

Makes 10 pizza cups

Prep Time: 10 minutes • Cook Time: 25 minutes

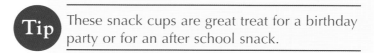

Tip These snack cups are great treat for a birthday party or for an after school snack.

pizza snack cups

funny face pizzas

1 package (10 ounces) refrigerated pizza dough
1 cup pizza sauce
1 cup (4 ounces) shredded mozzarella cheese
Assorted toppings: pepperoni, black olive slices, green or red bell pepper slices, mushroom slices
⅓ cup shredded Cheddar cheese

Heat oven to 425°F. Spray baking sheet with nonstick cooking spray; set aside.

Remove dough from package. *Do not unroll dough.* Slice dough into 4 equal pieces. Knead each piece of dough until ball forms. Pat or roll each ball into 4-inch disk. Place disks on prepared baking sheet.

Spread ¼ cup sauce on each disk. Sprinkle with mozzarella cheese. Decorate with assorted toppings to create faces. Sprinkle with Cheddar cheese to resemble hair.

Bake 10 minutes or until cheese is just melted and bottoms of pizzas are light brown.

Makes 4 servings

funny face pizza

sweet and sour chicken nuggets

2 (1-cup) bags UNCLE BEN'S® Boil-In-Bag Rice
1 package (10 ounces) frozen chicken nuggets or chicken chunks
1 tablespoon oil
2 large green bell peppers, cut into 1-inch squares
2 large carrots, diagonally cut into thin slices
1½ teaspoons minced garlic
2 cans (8 ounces each) pineapple chunks in juice, drained and ½ cup juice reserved
1 jar (10 ounces) sweet and sour sauce

1. Cook rice according to package directions.

2. Prepare chicken nuggets according to package directions for conventional oven.

3. Heat oil in large skillet over medium-high heat until hot. Add bell peppers, carrots and garlic; cook and stir 4 minutes. Add reserved pineapple juice. Cover; reduce heat and simmer 10 to 12 minutes until vegetables are almost tender. Add pineapple chunks; cover and cook 2 minutes. Stir in sweet and sour sauce; cover and cook 2 more minutes or until hot.

4. Place warm chicken nuggets on a bed of rice and top with vegetable mixture.

Makes 4 servings

magnificent salsa meatball hoagies

1 (6.8-ounce) package RICE-A-RONI® Beef Flavor
1 pound ground beef
½ cup dry bread crumbs
1 (24-ounce) jar salsa, divided
1 large egg
6 hoagie or French rolls, split in half
  Grated Parmesan cheese (optional)

1. In large bowl, combine rice-vermicelli mix, ground beef, bread crumbs, ½ cup salsa, egg and Special Seasonings. Shape meat mixture into 24 (1½-inch) meatballs. Arrange in large skillet.

2. Add 1½ cups water and remaining salsa; bring to a boil. Reduce heat to medium. Cover; simmer 30 to 35 minutes or until rice in meatballs is tender.

3. Place 4 meatballs in each roll. Top with sauce and cheese, if desired.

Makes 6 servings

Tip: For an Italian flair, use spaghetti sauce instead of salsa.

Prep Time: 15 minutes • Cook Time: 35 minutes

Meals on the Go

kids' quesadillas

  8 slices American cheese
  8 (10-inch) flour tortillas
  6 tablespoons *French's*® Sweet & Tangy Honey Mustard
  ½ pound thinly sliced deli turkey
  2 tablespoons melted butter
  ¼ teaspoon paprika

1. To prepare 1 quesadilla, arrange 2 slices of cheese on 1 tortilla. Top with one-fourth of the turkey. Spread with *1½ tablespoons* mustard, then top with another tortilla. Prepare 3 more quesadillas with remaining ingredients.

2. Combine butter and paprika. Brush one side of tortilla with butter mixture. Preheat 12-inch nonstick skillet over medium-high heat. Arrange tortilla butter side down and cook 2 minutes. Brush tortilla with butter mixture and turn over. Cook 1½ minutes or until golden brown. Repeat with remaining three quesadillas.

3. Slice into wedges before serving.

Makes 4 servings

Prep Time: 5 minutes • Cook Time: 15 minutes

kids quesadillas

celtic knots

1 package (16 ounces) hot roll mix plus ingredients to prepare mix
1 egg white
2 teaspoons water
2 tablespoons coarse salt

1. Prepare hot roll mix according to package directions.

2. Preheat oven to 375°F. Lightly grease baking sheets; set aside.

3. Divide dough equally into 16 pieces; shape each piece into 10-inch rope. Form each rope into interlocking ring as shown in photo; place on prepared baking sheets. Moisten ends of rope at seams; pinch to seal.

4. Beat egg white and water in small bowl until foamy. Brush onto dough shapes; sprinkle with coarse salt.

5. Bake about 15 minutes or until golden brown. Serve warm or at room temperature.

Makes about 18 knots

cartoona sandwiches

½ cup low fat mayonnaise
½ cup plain low fat yogurt
1½ teaspoons curry powder (optional)
1 cup SUN-MAID® Raisins or Fruit Bits
½ cup diced celery, or red or green bell pepper
1 green onion thinly sliced
1 large can (12 ounces) tuna packed in water, or substitute 1¼ cups chopped cooked chicken (two small chicken breasts)
6 sandwich rolls, round or oblong shaped

1. **MAKE FILLING:** Mix in a medium bowl, the mayonnaise, yogurt, curry powder, if desired, Sun-Maid® Raisins or Fruit Bits, celery or bell pepper, and green onion. Stir in tuna or chicken.

2. **MAKE "CAR":** Cut* a ½-inch slice off the top of a roll. With fingers or a fork, scoop out bread from center of roll.

3. **ATTACH** Sun-Maid® Apricots, carrot slices or other round ingredient to a toothpick to make car "wheels." Insert wheels into bottom edge of roll. Add apple slices for "fenders," if desired.

4. **MAKE** "headlights" using toothpicks to attach raisins on one end of the roll. Cut "doors" in sides of roll, if desired.

5. **FILL** roll with about ½ cup tuna or chicken salad. Place roll top on top of "car." Repeat with remaining rolls.

Makes 6 sandwiches

*Adult Supervision Suggested

Tip: Remove all toothpicks before eating.

Prep Time: 20 minutes

peanut butter and jelly club sandwich

3 tablespoons JIF® Creamy Peanut Butter
3 slices bread
2 tablespoons SMUCKER'S® Strawberry Jam
½ banana, sliced
2 strawberries, sliced

1. Spread JIF® peanut butter on 2 slices of bread. Spread SMUCKER'S® Strawberry Jam on the remaining slice of bread.

2. Place sliced banana on top of 1 slice of bread with JIF® peanut butter. Place sliced strawberries on top of other piece of bread with JIF® peanut butter.

3. Put piece of bread with strawberries on top of bread with bananas. Close sandwich with slice of bread with SMUCKER'S® Strawberry Jam facing down.   *Makes 1 serving*

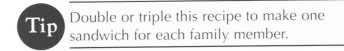

Tip Double or triple this recipe to make one sandwich for each family member.

turkey and macaroni

    1 teaspoon vegetable oil
1½ pounds ground turkey
    2 cans (10¾ ounces each) condensed tomato soup, undiluted
    2 cups uncooked macaroni, cooked and drained
    1 can (16 ounces) corn, drained
    ½ cup chopped onion
    1 can (4 ounces) sliced mushrooms, drained
    2 tablespoons ketchup
    1 tablespoon mustard
    Salt and black pepper to taste

SLOW COOKER DIRECTIONS

Heat oil in medium skillet; cook turkey until browned. Transfer mixture to slow cooker. Add remaining ingredients to slow cooker. Stir to blend. Cover; cook on LOW 7 to 9 hours or on HIGH 3 to 4 hours.

Makes 4 to 6 servings

sweet treat tortillas

4 (7- to 8-inch) flour tortillas
4 ounces Neufchatel cheese, softened
¼ cup strawberry or other flavor spreadable fruit or preserves
1 medium banana, peeled and chopped

1. Spread each tortilla with 1 ounce Neufchatel cheese and 1 tablespoon spreadable fruit; top with ¼ of the banana.

2. Roll up tortillas; cut crosswise into thirds.   *Makes 6 servings*

Cinnamon-Spice Treats: Omit spreadable fruit and banana. Mix small amounts of sugar, ground cinnamon and nutmeg to taste into Neufchatel cheese; spread evenly onto tortillas. Sprinkle lightly with desired amount of chopped pecans or walnuts. Top with chopped fruit, if desired; roll up. Cut crosswise into thirds.

Tip Substitute your favorite chopped fruit for banana for some more sweet treats.

stuffed franks 'n' taters

   4 cups frozen hash brown potatoes, thawed
   1 can (10¾ ounces) condensed cream of celery soup
1⅓ cups *French's®* French Fried Onions, divided
   1 cup (4 ounces) shredded Cheddar cheese, divided
   1 cup sour cream
 ½ teaspoon salt
 ¼ teaspoon pepper
   6 frankfurters

Preheat oven to 400°F. In large bowl, combine potatoes, soup, ⅔ *cup* French Fried Onions, ½ *cup* cheese, sour cream and seasonings. Spread potato mixture in 12×8-inch baking dish. Split frankfurters lengthwise almost into halves. Arrange frankfurters, split-side up, along center of casserole. Bake, covered, at 400°F for 30 minutes or until heated through. Fill frankfurters with remaining cheese and ⅔ *cup* onions; bake, uncovered, 1 to 3 minutes or until onions are golden brown.   *Makes 6 servings*

Microwave Directions: Prepare potato mixture as above; spread in 12×8-inch microwave-safe dish. Cook, covered, on HIGH 8 minutes; stir potato mixture halfway through cooking time. Split frankfurters and arrange on potatoes as above. Cook, covered, 4 to 6 minutes or until frankfurters are heated through. Rotate dish halfway through cooking time. Fill frankfurters with remaining cheese and ⅔ *cup* onions; cook, uncovered, 1 minute or until cheese melts. Let stand 5 minutes.

trail mix bars

        3 cups crispy rice cereal
        3 cups toasted oat cereal
    1½ cups raisins
        ½ cup sunflower seeds
        1 cup honey
        ¾ cup sugar
        1 (18 ounce) jar JIF® Extra Crunchy Peanut Butter
        1 teaspoon vanilla

Combine cereal, raisins and sunflower seeds in large bowl.

Combine honey and sugar in medium pan; heat over medium heat 3 to 5 minutes or until mixture comes to a boil. Boil 1 minute.

Add JIF® peanut butter and vanilla; stir until JIF® is melted. Pour over cereal mixture; mix well.

Press mixture into greased 15×10×1-inch baking pan.

When cool, cut into 1½-inch bars.   *Makes 1 dozen bars*

Tip: Spray a measuring cup with CRISCO® Cooking Spray before adding peanut butter or honey. The ingredients will come out much easier.

Note: Trail Mix Bars are an ideal snack to keep on hand. The bars can even be a delicious and healthful breakfast-on the-run!

3-cheese chicken & noodles

3 cups chopped cooked chicken

1½ cups cottage cheese

1 can (10¾ ounces) condensed cream of chicken soup, undiluted

1 package (8 ounces) wide egg noodles, cooked and drained

1 cup grated Monterey Jack cheese

½ cup diced celery

½ cup diced onion

½ cup diced green bell pepper

½ cup diced red bell pepper

½ cup grated Parmesan cheese

½ cup chicken broth

1 can (4 ounces) sliced mushrooms, drained

2 tablespoons butter, melted

½ teaspoon dried thyme leaves

SLOW COOKER DIRECTIONS

Combine all ingredients in slow cooker. Stir to coat evenly. Cover; cook on LOW 6 to 10 hours or on HIGH 3 to 4 hours.   *Makes 6 servings*

103

3-cheese chicken
& noodles

rainbow spirals

   4 (10-inch) flour tortillas (assorted flavors and colors)
   4 tablespoons *French's®* Mustard (any flavor)
   ½ pound (about 8 slices) thinly sliced deli roast beef, bologna or turkey
   8 slices American, provolone or Muenster cheese
   Fancy Party Toothpicks

1. Spread each tortilla with *1 tablespoon* mustard. Layer with meat and cheeses dividing evenly.

2. Roll up jelly-roll style; secure with toothpicks and cut into thirds. Arrange on platter.

Makes 4 to 6 servings

Prep Time: 10 minutes

Tip These spirals are a fun snack for a picnic or lunchtime treat.

rainbow spirals

chocolate & fruit snack mix

½ cup (1 stick) butter or margarine
2 tablespoons sugar
1 tablespoon HERSHEY'S Cocoa or HERSHEY'S Dutch Processed Cocoa
½ teaspoon ground cinnamon
3 cups bite-size crisp rice squares cereal
3 cups bite-size crisp wheat squares cereal
2 cups toasted oat cereal rings
1 cup cashews
1½ cups (6-ounce package) dried fruit bits
1 cup HERSHEY'S Semi-Sweet Chocolate Chips

1. Place butter in 4-quart microwave-safe bowl. Microwave at HIGH (100%) 1 minute or until melted; stir in sugar, cocoa and cinnamon. Add cereals and cashews; stir until evenly coated. Microwave at HIGH 3 minutes, stirring after each minute; stir in dried fruit. Microwave at HIGH 3 minutes, stirring after each minute.

2. Cool completely; stir in chocolate chips. Store in tightly covered container in cool, dry place.   *Makes about 11 cups*

5-minute heat and go soup

    1 can (16 ounces) low-sodium navy beans, rinsed and drained
    1 can (14½ ounces) diced tomatoes with green peppers and onions
    1 cup water
 1½ teaspoons dried basil leaves
    ½ teaspoon sugar
    ½ teaspoon low-sodium chicken bouillon granules
    2 teaspoons olive oil

1. Place all ingredients, except oil, in medium saucepan. Bring to a boil over high heat. Reduce heat and simmer 5 minutes, uncovered. Remove from heat, stir in oil; serve.

2. If desired, to transport, place hot soup in vacuum flask or allow to cool and place in a plastic container. Reheat in microwave when needed.   *Makes 3½ cups (4 servings)*

smoked turkey tortilla roll-ups

    4 (10-inch) flour tortillas
    4 tablespoons *French's*® Sweet & Tangy Honey Mustard
    ½ pound sliced smoked turkey or ham
    1 cup shredded lettuce
    1 cup chopped tomatoes

1. Spread each flour tortilla with *1 tablespoon* mustard. Top with 2 slices turkey and ¼ cup *each* lettuce and tomatoes.

2. Roll up jelly-roll style. Wrap in plastic wrap; chill. Cut in half to serve.
    Makes 4 servings

Prep Time: 10 minutes

peanut butter and jelly pizza sandwich

1 English muffin
2 tablespoons JIF® Creamy Peanut Butter
2 tablespoons SMUCKER'S® Strawberry Jam
6 to 8 slices banana
   Chocolate syrup
   Sweetened, flaked coconut (optional)

1. Split and toast English muffin. Spread JIF® peanut butter on both sides of the English muffin. Spread SMUCKER'S® Strawberry Jam on JIF® peanut butter.

2. Top with banana slices. Drizzle on chocolate syrup to taste. Sprinkle with coconut flakes if desired. Eat while still warm.

Makes 1 serving

 Tip Have fun making this sandwich with your kids. They can them make funny faces or decorate them as they like.

109
peanut butter and
jelly pizza sandwich

double peanut clusters

1²/₃ cups (10-ounce package) REESE'S® Peanut Butter Chips
1 tablespoon shortening (do not use butter, margarine, spread or oil)
2 cups salted peanuts

1. Line cookie sheet with waxed paper.

2. Place peanut butter chips and shortening in large microwave-safe bowl. Microwave at HIGH (100%) 1½ minutes; stir until chips are melted and mixture is smooth. If necessary, microwave an additional 30 seconds until chips are melted when stirred. Stir in peanuts.

3. Drop by rounded teaspoons onto prepared cookie sheet. (Mixture may also be dropped into small paper candy cups.) Cool until set. Store in cool, dry place.

Makes about 2½ dozen clusters

Butterscotch Nut Clusters: Follow above directions, substituting 1²/₃ cups (10-ounce package) HERSHEY'S Butterscotch Chips for Peanut Butter Chips.

111
double peanut clusters

peanut butter and fruit pita pockets

1 large crisp apple, peeled, cored and finely diced
1 medium Bartlett pear, peeled, cored and finely diced
1½ teaspoons raisins
2 teaspoons orange juice
3 tablespoons super chunk peanut butter
4 large lettuce leaves or 8 large spinach leaves
2 whole wheat pitas, about 2 ounces each

1. Combine diced apples, pears and raisins with orange juice and hold for 5 minutes. Add peanut butter and mix well.

2. Wash and dry lettuce or spinach leaves on absorbent paper towels. Tear lettuce into pita size pieces.

3. Warm pita in toaster on lowest color setting. Cut pita in half, and carefully open each half to make a pocket.

4. Line each pocket with lettuce or spinach leaves and spoon in equal portions of fruit and peanut butter mixture. Serve and enjoy.   *Makes 4 snack portions or 2 meal portions*

Note: A delicious and fun snack kids of all ages can make and enjoy...Sh-h-h-h, it's super healthy!

Favorite recipe from **Chilean Fresh Fruit Association**

sassy southwestern veggie wraps

½ **cup diced zucchini**
½ **cup diced red or yellow bell pepper**
½ **cup frozen corn, thawed and drained**
 1 **jalapeño pepper,* seeded and chopped (optional)**
¾ **cup shredded reduced-fat Mexican cheese blend**
 3 **tablespoons prepared salsa or picante sauce**
 2 **(8-inch) fat-free flour tortillas**

*Jalapeño peppers can sting and irritate the skin; wear rubber gloves when handling peppers and do not touch eyes. Wash hands after handling.

1. Combine zucchini, bell pepper, corn and jalapeño pepper, if desired, in small bowl. Stir in cheese and salsa; mix well.

2. Soften tortillas according to package directions. Spoon vegetable mixture down center of tortillas, distributing evenly; roll up burrito-style. Serve wraps cold or warm.** Garnish as desired. *Makes 2 servings*

**To warm each wrap, cover loosely with plastic wrap and microwave at HIGH 40 to 45 seconds or until cheese is melted.

quick & easy meatball soup

1 package (15 to 18 ounces) frozen Italian sausage meatballs without sauce
2 cans (about 14 ounces each) Italian-style stewed tomatoes
2 cans (about 14 ounces each) beef broth
1 can (about 14 ounces) mixed vegetables
½ cup uncooked rotini or small macaroni
½ teaspoon dried oregano leaves

1. Thaw meatballs in microwave oven according to package directions.

2. Place remaining ingredients in large saucepan. Add meatballs. Bring to a boil. Reduce heat; cover and simmer 15 minutes or until pasta is tender.   *Makes 4 to 6 servings*

Tip In a hurry? This soup cooks up in a flash and is so easy to reheat. Make it in the morning and serve it for a super fast lunch.

cheesy quesadillas

½ **pound ground beef**
1 **medium onion, chopped**
¼ **teaspoon salt**
1 **can (4½ ounces) chopped green chilies, drained**
1 **jar (1 pound 10 ounces) RAGÚ® Robusto!™ Pasta Sauce**
8 **(6-inch) flour tortillas**
1 **tablespoon olive oil**
2 **cups shredded Cheddar and/or mozzarella cheese (about 8 ounces)**

1. Preheat oven to 400°F. In 12-inch skillet, brown ground beef with onion and salt over medium-high heat; drain. Stir in chilies and ½ cup Ragú Pasta Sauce; set aside.

2. Meanwhile, evenly brush one side of 4 tortillas with half of the olive oil. On cookie sheets, arrange tortillas, oil-side down. Evenly top with ½ of the cheese, beef filling, then remaining cheese. Top with remaining 4 tortillas, then brush tops with remaining oil.

3. Bake 10 minutes or until cheese is melted. To serve, cut each quesadilla into 4 wedges. Serve with remaining sauce, heated.   *Makes 4 servings*

Prep Time: 10 minutes • Cook Time: 15 minutes

cheesy quesadillas

spicy, fruity popcorn mix

   4 cups lightly salted popcorn
   2 cups corn cereal squares
1½ cups dried pineapple wedges
   1 package (6 ounces) dried fruit bits
     Butter-flavored nonstick cooking spray
   2 tablespoons sugar
   1 tablespoon ground cinnamon
   1 cup yogurt-covered raisins

1. Preheat oven to 350°F. Combine popcorn, cereal, pineapple and fruit bits in large bowl; mix lightly. Transfer to 15×10-inch jelly-roll pan. Spray mixture generously with cooking spray.

2. Combine sugar and cinnamon in small bowl. Sprinkle ½ of the sugar mixture over popcorn mixture; toss lightly to coat. Spray mixture again with additional cooking spray. Add remaining sugar mixture; mix lightly.

3. Bake snack mix 10 minutes, stirring after 5 minutes. Cool completely in pan on wire rack. Add raisins; mix lightly.

Makes 7 to 8 cups

119
spicy, fruity popcorn mix

pizza turnovers

5 ounces reduced-fat mild Italian bulk turkey sausage
½ cup prepared pizza sauce
1 package (10 ounces) refrigerated pizza dough
⅓ cup shredded reduced-fat Italian cheese blend (10 ounces)

1. Preheat oven to 425°F. Cook sausage in nonstick saucepan until browned, stirring with spoon to break up meat. Drain fat. Add pizza sauce. Cook and stir until hot.

2. Spray baking sheet with nonstick olive oil cooking spray. Unroll pizza dough onto baking sheet. Pat into 12×8-inch rectangle. Cut into 6 (4×4-inch) squares. Divide sausage mixture evenly among squares. Sprinkle with cheese. Lift one corner of each square and fold over filling to opposite corner, making triangle. Press edges with tines of fork to seal.

3. Bake 11 to 13 minutes or until golden brown. Serve immediately or follow directions for freezing and reheating. *Makes 6 servings*

Note: To freeze turnovers, remove to wire rack to cool 30 minutes. Individually wrap in plastic wrap; place in freezer container or plastic freezer bag and freeze. To reheat turnovers, preheat oven to 400°F. Unwrap turnovers. Place in ungreased baking pan. Cover loosely with foil. Bake 18 to 22 minutes or until hot. Or, place one turnover on a paper-towel-lined microwavable plate. Heat on DEFROST (30% power) 3 to 3½ minutes or until hot, turning once.

pizza turnovers

peanut butter granola bites

2 cups cornflakes cereal
1 cup quick oats, uncooked
⅔ cup seedless raisins
½ cup chunky peanut butter
½ cup egg substitute *or* **4 egg whites**
1 cup EQUAL® SPOONFUL*
1 tablespoon honey
2 teaspoons vanilla
1 teaspoon ground cinnamon

May substitute 24 packets EQUAL® sweetener.

- Combine cornflakes, oats and raisins in large bowl.

- Combine peanut butter and egg substitute in medium bowl. Stir in Equal®, honey, vanilla and cinnamon until well blended. Spoon over cereal mixture. Toss gently to combine. Let stand 5 minutes.

- Preheated oven to 350°F. Shape mixture into 1-inch balls. Place on lightly sprayed baking sheet. Bake 8 to 10 minutes or until lightly golden and set. Remove to wire racks to cool completely.   *Makes about 2½ dozen*

cocktail wraps

16 thin strips Cheddar cheese*
16 HILLSHIRE FARM® Lit'l Smokies, scored lengthwise into halves
1 can (8 ounces) refrigerated crescent roll dough
1 egg, beaten *or* **1 tablespoon milk**
Mustard

Or substitute Swiss, taco-flavored or other variety of cheese.

Preheat oven to 400°F.

Place 1 strip cheese inside score of each Lit'l Smokie. Separate dough into 8 triangles; cut each lengthwise into halves to make 16 triangles. Place 1 link on wide end of 1 dough triangle; roll up. Repeat with remaining links and dough triangles. Place links on baking sheet. Brush dough with egg. Bake 10 to 15 minutes.

Serve hot with mustard.

Makes 16 hors d'oeuvres

crunchy turkey pita pockets

1 cup diced cooked turkey or chicken breast or reduced-sodium deli turkey breast
½ cup packaged cole slaw mix
½ cup dried cranberries
¼ cup shredded carrots
2 tablespoons reduced-fat or fat-free mayonnaise
1 tablespoon honey mustard
2 whole wheat pita breads

1. Combine turkey, cole slaw mix, cranberries, carrots, mayonnaise and mustard in small bowl; mix well.

2. Cut pita breads in half; fill with turkey mixture.

Makes 2 servings

sub on the run

   2 hard rolls (2 ounces each), split into halves
   4 tomato slices
 14 turkey pepperoni slices
   2 ounces fat-free oven-roasted turkey breast
 ¼ cup (1 ounce) shredded part-skim mozzarella or reduced-fat sharp Cheddar cheese
   1 cup packaged coleslaw mix or shredded lettuce
 ¼ medium green bell pepper, thinly sliced (optional)
   2 tablespoons prepared fat-free Italian salad dressing

Top each of two bottom halves of rolls with 2 tomato slices, 7 pepperoni slices, half of turkey, 2 tablespoons cheese, ½ cup coleslaw mix and half of bell pepper slices, if desired. Drizzle with salad dressing. Top with roll tops. Cut into halves, if desired.

Makes 2 servings

 Tip The name says it all—this sandwich is perfect for lunch on the go.

spooky tortilla chips

    Salt to taste
  3 packages (12 ounces each) 8-inch plain or flavored flour tortillas
    Nonstick cooking spray

- Preheat oven to 350°F. Spray baking sheet with olive oil nonstick cooking spray.

- Using 3-inch Halloween cookie cutters, cut tortillas, one at a time, into shapes. Discard scraps.

- Lightly spray tortilla shapes with cooking spray. Place on prepared baking sheet and sprinkle with salt.

- Bake 5 to 7 minutes or until edges begin to brown. Remove to wire rack to cool completely.

Makes about 90 chips

take-along snack mix

  1 tablespoon butter or margarine
  2 tablespoons honey
  1 cup toasted oat cereal, any flavor
  1/2 cup coarsely broken pecans
  1/2 cup thin pretzel sticks, broken in half
  1/2 cup raisins
  1 cup "M&M's"® Chocolate Mini Baking Bits

In large heavy skillet over low heat, melt butter; add honey and stir until blended. Add cereal, nuts, pretzels and raisins, stirring until all pieces are evenly coated. Continue cooking over low heat about 10 minutes, stirring frequently. Remove from heat; immediately spread on waxed paper until cool. Add "M&M's"® Chocolate Mini Baking Bits. Store in tightly covered container.

Makes about 3 1/2 cups

Contents

Morning Munchies

granola crisp topping with fruit

- $\frac{1}{3}$ cup old-fashioned rolled oats, uncooked
- 3 tablespoons chopped walnuts
- $\frac{1}{4}$ cup honey
- 1 egg white
- $\frac{1}{4}$ teaspoon vanilla
- $\frac{1}{4}$ teaspoon ground cinnamon
- Dash salt
- 2 cups nonfat plain or vanilla yogurt
- 2 cups mixed berries

Combine oats and walnuts in medium bowl. Mix together honey, egg white, vanilla, cinnamon and salt in small bowl until well blended. Add honey mixture to oats; stir until well blended. Line 11×17-inch baking sheet with foil; spray with nonstick cooking spray. Spread oat mixture in even layer on prepared baking sheet. Bake at 325°F 15 to 17 minutes or until golden brown, tossing mixture 3 to 4 times during baking. Remove from oven. Cool completely until crisp and crunchy. Serve over yogurt and berries.   *Makes 4 servings*

Favorite recipe from **National Honey Board**

129
granola crisp
topping with fruit

fudgey peanut butter chip muffins

½ cup applesauce
½ cup quick-cooking rolled oats
¼ cup (½ stick) butter or margarine, softened
½ cup granulated sugar
½ cup packed light brown sugar
 1 egg
½ teaspoon vanilla extract
¾ cup all-purpose flour
¼ cup HERSHEY'S Dutch Processed Cocoa or HERSHEY'S Cocoa
½ teaspoon baking soda
¼ teaspoon ground cinnamon (optional)
 1 cup REESE'S® Peanut Butter Chips
   Powdered sugar (optional)

1. Heat oven to 350°F. Line muffin cups (2½ inches in diameter) with paper bake cups.

2. Stir together applesauce and oats in small bowl; set aside. Beat butter, granulated sugar, brown sugar, egg and vanilla in large bowl until well blended. Add applesauce mixture; blend well. Stir together flour, cocoa, baking soda and cinnamon, if desired. Add to butter mixture, blending well. Stir in peanut butter chips. Fill muffin cups ¾ full with batter.

3. Bake 22 to 26 minutes or until wooden pick inserted in center comes out almost clean. Cool slightly in pan on wire rack. Sprinkle muffin tops with powdered sugar, if desired. Serve warm. *Makes 12 to 15 muffins*

Fudgey Chocolate Chip Muffins: Omit Peanut Butter Chips. Add 1 cup HERSHEY'S Semi-Sweet Chocolate Chips.

131
fudgey peanut butter
chip muffins

harvest apple oatmeal

1 cup apple juice
1 cup water
1 medium apple, cored and chopped
1 cup uncooked old-fashioned oats
¼ cup raisins
⅛ teaspoon salt
⅛ teaspoon ground cinnamon

MICROWAVE DIRECTIONS

1. Combine juice, water and apple in 2-quart microwavable bowl. Microwave at HIGH (100%) 3 minutes, stirring halfway through cooking time.

2. Add oats, raisins, salt and cinnamon; stir until well blended.

3. Microwave at MEDIUM (50% power) 4 to 5 minutes or until thick; stir before serving.

Makes 2 servings

Conventional Directions: To prepare conventionally, bring apple juice, water and apple to a boil in medium saucepan over medium-high heat. Stir in oats, raisins, cinnamon and salt until well blended. Cook, uncovered, over medium heat 5 to 6 minutes or until thick, stirring occasionally.

strawberry muffins

1¼ cups all-purpose flour
2½ teaspoons baking powder
½ teaspoon salt
1 cup uncooked old-fashioned oats
½ cup sugar
1 cup milk
½ cup butter, melted
1 egg, beaten
1 teaspoon vanilla
1 cup chopped fresh strawberries

Preheat oven to 425°F. Grease 12 (2½-inch) muffin cups; set aside.

Combine flour, baking powder and salt in large bowl. Stir in oats and sugar. Combine milk, butter, egg and vanilla in small bowl until well blended; stir into flour mixture just until moistened. Fold in strawberries. Spoon into prepared muffin cups, filling about two-thirds full.

Bake 15 to 18 minutes or until lightly browned and toothpick inserted into centers comes out clean. Remove from pan. Cool on wire rack 10 minutes. Serve warm or cool completely.

Makes 12 muffins

Toll House® mini morsel pancakes

2½ cups all-purpose flour
1 cup (6 ounces) NESTLÉ® TOLL HOUSE® Semi-Sweet Chocolate Mini Morsels
1 tablespoon baking powder
½ teaspoon salt
1¾ cups milk
2 large eggs
⅓ cup vegetable oil
⅓ cup packed brown sugar
Powdered sugar
Fresh sliced strawberries
Maple syrup

COMBINE flour, morsels, baking powder and salt in large bowl. Combine milk, eggs, vegetable oil and brown sugar in medium bowl; add to flour mixture. Stir just until moistened (batter may be lumpy).

HEAT griddle or skillet over medium heat; brush lightly with vegetable oil. Pour ¼ *cup* of batter onto hot griddle; cook until bubbles begin to burst. Turn; continue to cook for about 1 minute longer or until golden. Repeat with *remaining* batter.

SPRINKLE with powdered sugar; top with strawberries. Serve with maple syrup.

Makes about 18 pancakes

135

Toll House® mini morsel pancakes

breakfast parfait

1 cup Date-Nut Granola (recipe follows) or your favorite granola
½ cup plain nonfat yogurt or low-fat (1%) cottage cheese
1 cup sliced strawberries
1 ripe banana, sliced

Place quarter of granola in one parfait glass or glass bowl. Top with quarter of yogurt. Arrange quarter of strawberries and half banana over yogurt. Top with quarter of remaining granola, yogurt and strawberries. Repeat with remaining ingredients and parfait glass.

Makes 2 servings

date-nut granola

2 cups uncooked old-fashioned oats
2 cups barley flakes
1 cup sliced almonds
⅓ cup vegetable oil
⅓ cup honey
1 teaspoon vanilla
1 cup chopped dates

1. Preheat oven to 350°F. Grease 13×9-inch baking pan.

2. Combine oats, barley flakes and almonds in large bowl; set aside.

3. Combine oil, honey and vanilla in small bowl. Pour honey mixture over oat mixture; stir well. Pour into prepared pan.

4. Bake about 25 minutes or until toasted, stirring frequently after the first 10 minutes. Stir in dates while mixture is still hot. Cool. Store tightly covered.

Makes 6 cups

berry loaf

2 cups all-purpose flour
1 cup sugar
1½ teaspoons baking powder
1 teaspoon salt
½ teaspoon baking soda
¾ cup orange juice
1 teaspoon freshly grated orange peel
2 tablespoons shortening
1 egg, slightly beaten
1 cup chopped fresh cranberries
1 cup HERSHEY'S MINI CHIPS™ Semi-Sweet Chocolate Chips
¾ cup chopped nuts
Powdered Sugar Glaze (page 139, optional)

1. Heat oven to 350°F. Grease 9×5×3-inch loaf pan.

2. Stir together flour, sugar, baking powder, salt and baking soda in large bowl. Add orange juice, orange peel, shortening and egg; stir until well blended. Stir in cranberries, small chocolate chips and nuts. Pour batter into prepared pan.

3. Bake 1 hour 5 minutes to 1 hour 10 minutes or until wooden pick inserted in center comes out clean. Cool 10 minutes; remove from pan to wire rack. Prepare Powdered Sugar Glaze, if desired; spread over top of loaf. Cool completely. Garnish as desired.

Makes 1 loaf (14 servings)

powdered sugar glaze

    1 cup powdered sugar
    1 tablespoon milk, plus more if needed
    1 teaspoon butter or margarine, softened
    ½ teaspoon vanilla extract

Stir together powdered sugar, milk, butter and vanilla in small bowl; beat until smooth and of desired consistency. Add additional milk, 1 teaspoon at a time, if needed.

Makes about ½ cup glaze

apple raisin pancakes

    2 cups all-purpose flour
    2 tablespoons sugar
    1 tablespoon baking powder
    2 teaspoons ground cinnamon
  1¾ cups fat-free (skim) milk
    ⅔ cup EGG BEATERS®
    5 tablespoons FLEISCHMANN'S® Original Margarine, melted, divided
    ¾ cup chopped apple
    ¾ cup seedless raisins

In large bowl, combine flour, sugar, baking powder and cinnamon. In medium bowl, combine milk, Egg Beaters® and 4 tablespoons margarine; stir into dry ingredients just until blended. Stir in apple and raisins.

Brush large nonstick griddle or skillet with some of remaining margarine; heat over medium-high heat. Using ¼ cup batter for each pancake, pour batter onto griddle. Cook until bubbly; turn and cook until lightly browned. Repeat with remaining batter, using remaining margarine as needed, to make 16 pancakes. *Makes 16 (4-inch) pancakes*

Prep Time: 10 minutes • Cook Time: 15 minutes

apple cinnamon quesadillas

Spiced Yogurt Dipping Sauce (recipe follows)
1 medium McIntosh apple, cored and chopped
¾ cup no-sugar-added applesauce
⅛ teaspoon ground cinnamon
4 (6-inch) flour tortillas
¼ cup (1 ounce) shredded reduced-fat Cheddar cheese
Nonstick cooking spray

1. Prepare Spiced Yogurt Dipping Sauce; set aside.

2. Combine apple, applesauce and cinnamon in small bowl; mix well.

3. Spoon half of apple mixture onto tortilla; sprinkle with half of cheese. Top with another tortilla. Repeat with remaining tortillas, apple mixture and cheese.

4. Spray large nonstick skillet with cooking spray; heat over medium heat until hot. Cook quesadillas, one at a time, about 2 minutes on each side or until golden brown. Cut each quesadilla into four wedges. Serve with Spiced Yogurt Dipping Sauce.   *Makes 4 servings*

spiced yogurt dipping sauce

½ cup vanilla-flavored low-fat yogurt
2 tablespoons no-sugar-added applesauce
Dash ground cinnamon

Combine yogurt, applesauce and cinnamon in small bowl; mix well. Refrigerate until ready to use.

141
apple cinnamon
quesadillas

oat cakes with fresh fruit topping

　1 pint hulled strawberries, raspberries or blueberries, divided
　½ cup sugar, divided
　2 tablespoons cornstarch
　½ cup water
　1 teaspoon lemon juice
　½ cup uncooked oats
　1 cup whole wheat flour
2½ teaspoons baking powder
1¼ cups fat-free (skim) milk
　½ cup plain nonfat yogurt
　　Nonstick cooking spray

Place half of strawberries in medium bowl; mash with potato masher. Slice remaining strawberries; set aside. (If using raspberries or blueberries, do not slice.)

Combine ⅓ cup sugar and cornstarch in small saucepan. Stir in water until cornstarch is dissolved. Cook and stir over medium heat until mixture comes to a boil. Add lemon juice and mashed strawberries; return to a boil. Remove from heat; let stand 15 minutes. Stir in sliced strawberries.

Stir oats in heavy skillet over medium heat 3 minutes or until slightly browned. Turn into medium bowl; cool 10 minutes. Stir in flour, baking powder and remaining sugar. Combine milk and yogurt in small bowl; stir into flour mixture just until all ingredients are moistened. (Batter will be lumpy.)

Coat nonstick griddle or heavy skillet with nonstick cooking spray. Heat over medium heat until water droplets sprinkled on griddle bounce off surface. Drop batter by scant ¼ cupfuls onto griddle; spread batter to form 4-inch round cakes. Cook 2 minutes or until bubbles appear on entire top of batter. Turn cakes; cook 2 minutes longer or until browned. Serve warm with fruit sauce.　　　*Makes 6 servings (2 oat cakes and ⅓ cup sauce per serving)*

oat cakes with fresh
fruit topping

breakfast kabobs

2 cups plain yogurt
4 tablespoons honey
1 (12-ounce) package BOB EVANS® Original or Maple Links
1 medium cantaloupe melon, peeled, seeded and cut into 1-inch cubes
1 medium honeydew melon, peeled, seeded and cut into 1-inch cubes
1 small bunch green seedless grapes
1 small bunch red seedless grapes
2 medium red apples, cored and cut into 1-inch cubes
1 pint strawberries, hulled and cut into halves

Combine yogurt and honey in small bowl; refrigerate until ready to serve. Cook sausage in medium skillet over medium heat until browned. Drain on paper towels; cut each link in half. Alternately place sausage and fruit on wooden skewers (about 7). Serve kabobs with yogurt sauce for dipping.

Makes about 7 kabobs

Tip The fruit can be prepared ahead and refrigerated until ready to assemble kabobs with warm sausage. Brush apples with lemon or orange juice to prevent discoloration.

breakfast kabobs

cinnamon-raisin rolls

    1 package (16 ounces) hot roll mix plus ingredients to prepare mix
$\frac{1}{3}$ cup raisins
    4 tablespoons butter, softened and divided
$\frac{1}{4}$ cup granulated sugar
    2 teaspoons ground cinnamon
$\frac{1}{2}$ teaspoon ground nutmeg
$1\frac{1}{2}$ cups powdered sugar
    1 to 2 tablespoons fat-free (skim) milk
$\frac{1}{2}$ teaspoon vanilla

1. Preheat oven to 375°F. Spray 13×9-inch baking pan with nonstick cooking spray.

2. Prepare hot roll mix according to package directions; mix in raisins. Knead dough on lightly floured surface until smooth and elastic, about 5 minutes. Cover dough with plastic wrap; let stand 5 minutes.

3. Roll out dough on floured surface to 16×10-inch rectangle. Spread dough with 2 tablespoons butter. Combine granulated sugar, cinnamon and nutmeg in small bowl; sprinkle evenly over dough. Roll up dough starting at long end. Pinch edge of dough to seal.

4. Gently stretch sealed dough until 18 inches long. Cut dough into 1-inch pieces; place, cut side up, in prepared pan. Cover pan loosely with towel. Let stand 20 to 30 minutes or until doubled in size.

5. Bake 20 to 25 minutes or until golden. Cool in pan on wire rack 2 to 3 minutes. Remove from pan; cool on wire rack.

6. To make glaze, combine powdered sugar, remaining 2 tablespoons butter, 1 tablespoon milk and vanilla in medium bowl. Add additional 1 tablespoon milk to make thinner glaze, if needed. Spread glaze over warm rolls. *Makes 1½ dozen rolls*

cinnamon-raisin rolls

bunny pancakes with strawberry butter

  Strawberry Butter (recipe follows)
2 cups buttermilk baking mix
1 cup milk
2 eggs
½ cup plain yogurt
  Assorted candies

1. Prepare Strawberry Butter; set aside. Preheat electric skillet or griddle to 375°F.

2. Combine baking mix, milk, eggs and yogurt in medium bowl; mix well. Spoon scant ½ cup batter into skillet. With back of spoon, gently spread batter into 4-inch circle. Spoon about 2 tablespoons batter onto top edge of circle for head. Using back of spoon, spread batter from head to form bunny ears as shown in photo.

3. Cook until bubbles on surface begin to pop and top of pancake appears dry; turn pancake over. Cook until done, 1 to 2 minutes. Decorate with candies as shown in photo.

4. Repeat with remaining batter. Serve warm with Strawberry Butter.

Makes about 12 (8-inch) pancakes

Reindeer Pancakes: Prepare batter as directed. Spoon scant ¼ cup batter into skillet. Quickly spread batter with back of spoon to form antlers as shown in photo. Cook as directed. Decorate as shown in photo. Serve as directed.

strawberry butter

1 package (3 ounces) cream cheese, softened
½ cup butter, softened
⅓ cup powdered sugar
1½ cups fresh or thawed frozen strawberries

Place cream cheese and butter in food processor or blender; process until smooth. Add sugar; process until blended. Add strawberries; process until finely chopped.   *Makes about 1⅓ cups*

149

clockwise from right: reindeer
pancake, bunny pancake
and strawberry butter

breakfast cookies

1 Butter Flavor CRISCO® Stick or 1 cup Butter Flavor CRISCO® All-Vegetable Shortening

1 cup JIF® Extra Crunchy Peanut Butter

¾ cup granulated sugar

¾ cup firmly packed brown sugar

2 eggs, beaten

1½ cups all-purpose flour

1 teaspoon baking powder

1 teaspoon baking soda

1 teaspoon ground cinnamon

1¾ cups quick oats, uncooked

1¼ cups raisins

1 medium Granny Smith apple, finely grated, including juice

⅓ cup finely grated carrot

¼ cup flake coconut (optional)

Preheat oven to 350°F. Place sheets of foil on countertop for cooling cookies.

Combine 1 cup shortening, JIF® peanut butter and sugars in large bowl. Beat at medium speed with electric mixer until blended. Beat in eggs.

Combine flour, baking powder, baking soda and cinnamon. Add gradually to creamed mixture at low speed. Beat until blended. Sir in oats, raisins, apple, carrot and coconut. Drop by tablespoonfuls onto ungreased baking sheet.

Bake for 9 to 11 minutes or until just browned around edges. Do not overbake. Cool 2 minutes on baking sheet. Remove cookies to foil to cool completely.

Makes 5 to 6 dozen cookies

Tip: Freeze cookies between sheets of waxed paper in sealed container. Use as needed for breakfast on-the-run or as a nutritious snack.

harvest mini chip muffins

    1 cup sugar
    ¼ cup (½ stick) butter or margarine
    1 cup canned pumpkin
    2 eggs
  2¼ cups all-purpose flour
    2 teaspoons baking powder
    ¾ teaspoon pumpkin pie spice
    ½ teaspoon baking soda
    ½ teaspoon salt
    ½ cup milk
    1 cup HERSHEY'S MINI CHIPS™ Semi-Sweet Chocolate Chips
    ½ cup chopped pecans

1. Heat oven to 350°F. Grease or line muffin cups (2½ inches in diameter) with paper bake cups.

2. Beat sugar and butter in large bowl until creamy. Add pumpkin and eggs; blend well. Stir together flour, baking powder, pumpkin pie spice, baking soda and salt; add alternately with milk to pumpkin mixture, beating after each addition just until blended. Stir in mini chocolate chips and pecans. Fill muffin cups ⅔ full with batter.

3. Bake 20 to 25 minutes or until wooden pick inserted in center comes out clean. Serve warm.

Makes about 2 dozen muffins

silver dollar pancakes with mixed berry topping

1¼ cups all-purpose flour
2 tablespoons sugar
2 teaspoons baking soda
1½ cups buttermilk
½ cup EGG BEATERS®
3 tablespoons FLEISCHMANN'S® Original Margarine, melted, divided
Mixed Berry Topping (recipe follows)

In large bowl, combine flour, sugar and baking soda. Stir in buttermilk, Egg Beaters® and 2 tablespoons margarine just until blended.

Brush large nonstick griddle or skillet with some of remaining margarine; heat over medium-high heat. Using 1 heaping tablespoon batter for each pancake, spoon batter onto griddle. Cook until bubbly; turn and cook until lightly browned. Repeat with remaining batter using remaining margarine as needed to make 28 pancakes. Serve hot with Mixed Berry Topping.

Makes 28 (2-inch) pancakes

Mixed Berry Topping: In medium saucepan, over medium-low heat, combine 1 (12-ounce) package frozen mixed berries,* thawed, ¼ cup honey and ½ teaspoon grated gingerroot (or ⅛ teaspoon ground ginger). Cook and stir just until hot and well blended. Serve over pancakes. *Three cups mixed fresh berries may be substituted.*

Prep Time: 20 minutes • Cook Time: 20 minutes

strawberry cinnamon french toast

1 large egg
¼ cup fat-free (skim) milk
½ teaspoon vanilla
4 (1-inch-thick) diagonally cut slices French bread (about 1 ounce each)
2 teaspoons reduced-fat margarine
2 packets sugar substitute
¼ teaspoon ground cinnamon
1 cup sliced strawberries
Fresh mint leaves, for garnish (optional)

1. Preheat oven to 450°F.

2. Spray nonstick baking sheet with nonstick cooking spray; set aside.

3. Combine egg, milk and vanilla in shallow dish or pie plate. Lightly dip bread slices in egg mixture until completely coated. Place on baking sheet; bake 15 minutes or until golden.

4. Meanwhile, combine margarine, sugar substitute and cinnamon in small bowl; stir until well blended. Spread mixture evenly over French toast. Top with strawberries.

Makes 4 servings

Prep Time: 10 minutes • Bake Time: 15 minutes

155

strawberry cinnamon
french toast

wafflewich

2 frozen cinnamon waffles
25 miniature marshmallows
2 tablespoons JIF® Creamy Peanut Butter
½ banana, sliced
¼ cup chocolate chips

1. Toast waffles in the toaster until desired darkness.

2. Heat miniature marshmallows and JIF® in microwave until melted, then mix together.

3. Spread the JIF® peanut butter mixture on waffle.

4. Place banana slices on JIF® peanut butter mixture.

5. Top with chocolate chips.

6. Close sandwich with other waffle.

7. It tastes better warm!

Makes 1 wafflewich

hearty banana carrot muffins

2 ripe, medium DOLE® Bananas
1 package (14 ounces) oat bran muffin mix
¾ teaspoon ground ginger
1 medium DOLE® Carrot, shredded (½ cup)
⅓ cup light molasses
⅓ cup DOLE® Seedless or Golden Raisins
¼ cup chopped almonds

- Mash bananas with fork (1 cup).

- Combine muffin mix and ginger in large bowl. Add carrot, molasses, raisins and bananas. Stir just until moistened.

- Spoon batter into paper-lined muffin cups. Sprinkle tops with almonds.

- Bake at 425°F 12 to 14 minutes until browned.   *Makes 12 muffins*

Prep Time: 20 minutes • Bake Time: 14 minutes

chocolate brunch waffles

2¼ cups all-purpose flour
½ cup granulated sugar
1 tablespoon baking powder
¾ teaspoon salt
1 cup (6 ounces) NESTLÉ® TOLL HOUSE® Semi-Sweet Chocolate Morsels
¾ cup (1½ sticks) butter or margarine
1½ cups milk
3 large eggs, lightly beaten
1 tablespoon vanilla extract
Toppings (whipped cream, chocolate shavings, sifted powdered sugar, fresh fruit, ice cream)

COMBINE flour, sugar, baking powder and salt in large bowl.

MICROWAVE morsels and butter in medium, uncovered, microwave-safe bowl on HIGH (100%) power for 1 minute. STIR. Morsels may retain some of their original shape. If necessary, microwave at additional 10- to 15-second intervals, stirring just until morsels are melted. Cool to room temperature. Stir in milk, eggs and vanilla extract. Add chocolate mixture to flour mixture; stir (batter will be thick).

COOK in Belgian waffle maker* according to manufacturer's directions. Serve warm with your choice of toppings.   *Makes 10 Belgian waffle squares*

Can also be cooked in standard waffle maker (makes about 20 standard-size waffle squares).

Dynamite Dinners

monstrous mac & cheese

   2 packages (7 ounces each) macaroni & cheese mix
   4 slices pepperoni
     Pimiento-stuffed green olives
     Ripe olives
     Red, green and/or yellow bell peppers

1. Prepare macaroni and cheese according to directions. Transfer to four shallow bowls.

2. Cut pepperoni, olives and peppers into strips and shapes. Arrange over macaroni for monster faces.

Makes 4 servings

monstrous mac & cheese

make your own pizza shapes

1 package (10 ounces) refrigerated pizza dough
¼ to ½ cup prepared pizza sauce
1 cup shredded mozzarella cheese
1 cup *French's*® French Fried Onions

1. Preheat oven to 425°F. Unroll dough onto greased baking sheet. Press or roll dough into 12×8-inch rectangle. With sharp knife or pizza cutter, cut dough into large shape of your choice (butterfly, heart, star). Reroll scraps and cut into mini shapes. (See tip.)

2. Pre-bake crust 7 minutes or until crust just begins to brown. Spread with sauce and top with cheese. Bake 6 minutes or until crust is deep golden brown.

3. Sprinkle with French Fried Onions. Bake 2 minutes longer or until golden.

Makes 4 to 6 servings

Tip: Pizza dough can be cut with 6-inch shaped cookie cutters. Spread with sauce and top with cheese. Bake about 10 minutes or until crust is golden. Sprinkle with French Fried Onions. Bake 2 minutes longer.

Prep Time: 10 minutes • Cook Time: 15 minutes

make your own
pizza shapes

chubby chickers

    4 to 5 boneless, skinless chicken breast halves (1 to 1¼ pounds)
    1 package (4 ounces) shredded mozzarella cheese
      CRISCO® Butter Flavor No-Stick Cooking Spray
   ¾ cup all-purpose flour
    2 eggs
    2 tablespoons water
 2½ cups crushed pizza-flavored tortilla chips (¾ of 14½ ounce bag)
    1 can (15 ounces) pizza sauce, warmed

Heat oven to 450°F.

Rinse chicken; pat dry. Cut each breast half into 4 pieces. Make slit in each piece to form pocket. Stuff about 1 tablespoon cheese into each pocket, pressing closed with fingers.

Spray 15×10-inch jelly-roll pan with Crisco® Butter Flavor No-Stick Cooking Spray.

Place flour in medium bowl or on waxed paper. Combine eggs and water in small bowl. Beat well. Place crushed chips in pie plate or on waxed paper. Dip chicken pieces in flour, then in egg mixture and then in chips, pressing to coat well. Place on jelly-roll pan. Spray tops with cooking spray.

Bake for 12 to 15 minutes or until chicken is no longer pink in center. *Do not overbake.* Cool in pan on rack 5 minutes. Serve with warm pizza sauce for dipping.

Makes 16 pieces

taco cups

 1 pound lean ground beef, turkey or pork
 1 package (1 ounce) LAWRY'S® Taco Spices & Seasonings
 1¼ cups water
 ¼ cup salsa
 2 packages (8 ounces each) refrigerator biscuits
 ½ cup (2 ounces) shredded cheddar cheese

In medium skillet, brown ground beef until crumbly; drain fat. Stir in Taco Spices & Seasonings and water. Bring to a boil; reduce heat to low and cook, uncovered, 10 minutes. Stir in salsa. Separate biscuits and press each biscuit into an ungreased muffin cup. Spoon equal amounts of meat mixture into each muffin cup; sprinkle each with cheese. Bake, uncovered, in 350°F oven for 12 minutes. *Makes about 16 taco cups*

Prep. Time: 10 to 12 minutes • Cook Time: 22 to 27 minutes

sweet and sour hot dog bites

¼ cup prepared mustard
½ cup SMUCKER'S® Grape Jelly
1 tablespoon sweet pickle relish
½ pound frankfurters, cooked

In a saucepan, combine mustard, SMUCKER'S® jelly, and relish.

Heat over very low heat, stirring constantly, until mixture is hot and well blended.

Slice frankfurters diagonally into bite-size pieces. Add to sauce and heat thoroughly.

Makes 20 snack servings

easy frank & cheese pasta twists

2 cans (10¾ ounces each) condensed Cheddar cheese soup
2 cups milk
1 cup shredded sharp Cheddar cheese
1 package (16 ounces) rotini pasta, cooked and drained
4 beef frankfurters, cut into ½-inch-thick slices
1⅓ cups *French's*® French Fried Onions, divided

1. Preheat oven to 350°F. Mix soup and milk in medium saucepan; stir in cheese and cook until cheese melts, stirring frequently.

2. Combine pasta, frankfurters, ⅔ *cup* French Fried Onions and soup mixture in lightly greased shallow 3-quart baking dish.

3. Bake 30 minutes or until hot and bubbly. Stir. Top with remaining onions; bake 5 minutes or until onions are golden.

Makes 8 servings

Prep Time: 15 minutes • Cook Time: 35 minutes

sweet and sour
hot dog bites

hot dog macaroni

1 package (8 ounces) hot dogs
1 cup uncooked corkscrew pasta
1 cup shredded Cheddar cheese
1 box (10 ounces) BIRDS EYE® frozen Green Peas
1 cup 1% milk

• Slice hot dogs into bite-size pieces; set aside.

• In large saucepan, cook pasta according to package directions; drain and return to saucepan.

• Stir in hot dogs, cheese, peas and milk. Cook over medium heat 10 minutes or until cheese is melted, stirring occasionally. *Makes 4 servings*

Prep Time: 10 minutes • Cook Time: 20 minutes

169
hot dog macaroni

school night chicken rice taco toss

1 (6.9-ounce) package RICE-A-RONI® Chicken Flavor
2 tablespoons margarine or butter
1 (16-ounce) jar salsa
1 pound boneless, skinless chicken breasts, chopped
1 cup frozen or canned corn, drained
4 cups shredded lettuce
½ cup (2 ounces) shredded Cheddar cheese
2 cups tortilla chips, coarsely broken
1 medium tomato, chopped

1. In large skillet over medium-high heat, sauté rice-vermicelli mix with margarine until vermicelli is golden brown.

2. Slowly stir in 2 cups water, salsa, chicken and Special Seasonings. Bring to a boil. Reduce heat to low. Cover; simmer 10 minutes.

3. Stir in corn. Cover; simmer 5 to 10 minutes or until rice is tender and chicken is no longer pink.

4. Arrange lettuce on large serving platter. Top with chicken-rice mixture. Sprinkle with cheese and tortilla chips. Garnish with tomato.   *Makes 6 servings*

Prep Time: 10 minutes • Cook Time: 30 minutes

sweet & sour nugget kabobs

   1 package (12 ounces) refrigerated chicken nuggets
   1 can (8 ounces) pineapple chunks, drained
   1 green or red bell pepper, cut into 1-inch squares
   8 to 10 (6-inch) wooden skewers soaked in water
      Creamy Dip & Spread (recipe follows)

1. Preheat oven to 400°F. Alternately thread chicken nuggets, pineapple chunks and pepper squares onto skewers.

2. Arrange skewers on baking sheet. Bake 12 minutes or until heated through. Serve with **Creamy Dip & Spread** or your favorite *French's*® Mustard.   *Makes 4 servings*

Prep Time: 5 minutes • Cook Time: 12 minutes

creamy dip & spread

   ½ cup *French's*® Mustard (any flavor)
   ½ cup mayonnaise

Combine all ingredients in small bowl.   *Makes 1 cup*

Prep Time: 5 minutes

silly spaghetti casserole

8 ounces uncooked spaghetti, broken in half

¼ cup finely grated Parmesan cheese

¼ cup cholesterol-free egg substitute

½ (10-ounce) package frozen cut spinach, thawed and squeezed dry

¾ pound lean ground turkey or 90% lean ground beef

⅓ cup chopped onion

2 cups pasta sauce

¾ cup (3 ounces) shredded part-skim mozzarella cheese

1 green or yellow bell pepper, cored and seeded

1. Preheat oven to 350°F. Spray 8-inch square baking dish with nonstick cooking spray.

2. Cook spaghetti according to package directions, omitting salt and oil; drain. Return spaghetti to saucepan. Add Parmesan cheese and egg substitute; toss. Place in prepared baking dish.

3. Spray large nonstick skillet with cooking spray. Cook turkey and onion in skillet over medium-high heat until meat is lightly browned, stirring to break up meat. Drain fat from skillet. Stir in spinach and spaghetti sauce. Spoon on top of spaghetti mixture.

4. Sprinkle with mozzarella cheese. Use small cookie cutter to cut decorative shapes from bell pepper. Arrange on top of cheese. Cover with foil. Bake 40 to 45 minutes or until bubbling. Let stand 10 minutes. Cut into squares. *Makes 6 servings*

173
silly spaghetti casserole

mini chicken pot pies

    1 container (about 16 ounces) refrigerated reduced-fat buttermilk biscuits
1½ cups milk
    1 package (1.8 ounces) white sauce mix
    2 cups cut-up cooked chicken
    1 cup frozen assorted vegetables, partially thawed
    2 cups shredded Cheddar cheese
    2 cups *French's*® French Fried Onions

1. Preheat oven to 400°F. Separate biscuits; press into 8 (8-ounce) custard cups, pressing up sides to form crust.

2. Whisk milk and sauce mix in medium saucepan. Bring to boiling over medium-high heat. Reduce heat to medium-low; simmer 1 minute, whisking constantly, until thickened. Stir in chicken and vegetables.

3. Spoon about ⅓ cup chicken mixture into each crust. Place cups on baking sheet. Bake 15 minutes or until golden brown. Top each with cheese and French Fried Onions. Bake 3 minutes or until golden. To serve, remove from cups and transfer to serving plates.

Makes 8 servings

Prep Time: 15 minutes • Cook Time: about 20 minutes

mini chicken pot pie

kid kabobs with cheesy mustard dip

DIP

    1 container (8 ounces) whipped cream cheese
    ¼ cup milk
    3 tablespoons *French's*® Bold n' Spicy Brown Mustard or Sweet & Tangy Honey Mustard
    2 tablespoons mayonnaise
    2 tablespoons minced green onions

KABOBS

    ½ pound deli luncheon meat or cooked chicken and turkey, cut into 1-inch cubes
    ½ pound Swiss, Cheddar or Monterey Jack cheese, cut into 1-inch cubes
    2 cups cut-up assorted vegetables such as broccoli, carrots, peppers, cucumbers and celery
    16 wooden picks, about 6-inches long

1. Combine ingredients for dip in medium bowl; mix until well blended.

2. To make kabobs, place cubes of meat, cheese and chunks of vegetables on wooden picks.

3. Serve kabobs with dip.   *Makes 8 servings (about 1¼ cups dip)*

Prep Time: 15 minutes

golden chicken nuggets

1 envelope LIPTON® RECIPE SECRETS® Golden Onion Soup Mix
½ cup plain dry bread crumbs
1½ pounds boneless, skinless chicken breasts, cut into 2-inch pieces
2 tablespoons margarine or butter, melted

1. Preheat oven to 425°F. In small bowl, combine soup mix and bread crumbs. Dip chicken in bread crumb mixture until evenly coated.

2. On lightly greased cookie sheet, arrange chicken; drizzle with margarine.

3. Bake uncovered 15 minutes or until chicken is thoroughly cooked, turning once.

Makes 6 servings

Tip: Also terrific with Lipton® Recipe Secrets® Onion, Onion-Mushroom or Savory Herb with Garlic Soup Mix.

Prep Time: 10 minutes • Cook Time: 15 minutes

taco two-zies

1 pound ground beef
2 packages (1 ounce each) LAWRY'S® Taco Spices & Seasonings
¾ cup water
1 can (1 pound 14 ounces) refried beans, warmed
10 small flour tortillas (fajita size), warmed to soften
10 jumbo size taco shells, heated according to package directions

TACO TOPPINGS
Shredded lettuce, shredded cheddar cheese and chopped tomatoes

In large skillet, brown ground beef over medium high heat until crumbly; drain fat. Stir in 1 package Taco Spices & Seasonings and water. Bring to a boil; reduce heat to low and cook, uncovered, 10 minutes, stirring occasionally. In medium bowl, mix together beans and remaining package Taco Spices & Seasonings. Spread about ⅓-cup seasoned beans all the way to edges of each flour tortilla. Place a taco shell on center of each bean-tortilla and fold edges up around shell, lightly pressing to 'stick' tortilla to shell. Fill each taco with about 3 tablespoons taco meat. Top with your choice of taco toppings.   *Makes 10 tacos*

Variations: May use lean ground turkey, chicken or pork in place of ground beef. May use LAWRY'S® Chicken Taco Spices & Seasonings or Lawry's® Hot Taco Spices & Seasonings instead of Taco Spices & Seasonings.

Prep. Time: 8 to 10 minutes • Cook Time: 15 minutes

terrifying tamale pie

    1 tablespoon vegetable oil
$\frac{1}{2}$ cup chopped onion
$\frac{1}{3}$ cup chopped red bell pepper
    1 clove garlic, minced
$\frac{3}{4}$ pound ground turkey
$\frac{3}{4}$ teaspoon chili powder
$\frac{1}{2}$ teaspoon dried oregano leaves
    1 can (14$\frac{1}{2}$ ounces) Mexican-style stewed tomatoes, undrained
    1 can (15 ounces) chili beans in mild chili sauce, undrained
    1 cup corn
$\frac{1}{4}$ teaspoon black pepper
    1 package (8$\frac{1}{2}$ ounces) corn muffin mix plus ingredients to prepare mix
    2 cups taco-flavored shredded cheese, divided
      Green and red bell pepper, pickle slices, pimiento pieces, chopped onion, chopped
      black olives and carrots for decoration

1. Heat oil in large skillet over medium heat. Add onion and bell pepper; cook until crisp-tender. Stir in garlic. Add turkey; cook until turkey is no longer pink, stirring occasionally. Stir in chili powder and oregano. Add tomatoes with juice; cook and stir 2 minutes, breaking up tomatoes with spoon. Stir in beans with sauce, corn and black pepper; simmer 10 minutes or until liquid is reduced by about half.

2. Preheat oven to 375°F. Lightly grease 1$\frac{1}{2}$- to 2-quart casserole. Prepare corn muffin mix according to package directions; stir in $\frac{1}{2}$ cup cheese. Spread half of turkey mixture in prepared casserole; sprinkle with $\frac{3}{4}$ cup cheese. Top with remaining turkey mixture and $\frac{3}{4}$ cup cheese. Top with corn muffin batter. Decorate with assorted vegetables to make monster face. Bake 20 to 22 minutes or until light golden brown.   *Makes 6 to 8 servings*

Note: Make this pie cute instead of creepy by creating a simple jack-o'-lantern face with bell pepper cutouts.

terrifying tamale pie

cheesy chicken, coins & strings

    2 tablespoons margarine or butter
    1 pound boneless, skinless chicken breasts, cut into 1-inch pieces
    2 cups frozen crinkle-cut carrots
    ⅔ cup milk
    1 (4.8-ounce) package PASTA RONI® Angel Hair Pasta with Herbs
    ½ cup pasteurized processed cheese, cut into ½-inch cubes

1. In large skillet over medium-high heat, melt margarine. Add chicken; sauté 5 to 7 minutes or until chicken is no longer pink inside. Remove from skillet; set aside.

2. In same skillet, bring 1⅓ cups water, carrots and milk to a boil. Stir in pasta and Special Seasonings; return to a boil. Reduce heat to medium. Gently boil uncovered, 4 to 5 minutes or until pasta is tender, stirring frequently.

3. Stir in chicken and cheese. Let stand 3 minutes or until cheese is melted.

Makes 4 servings

Prep Time: 10 minutes • Cook Time: 15 minutes

triangle tostadas

   2 large (burrito size) flour tortillas
     Vegetable oil
   1 package (about 1 pound) lean ground pork
   1 package (1 ounce) LAWRY'S® Taco Spices & Seasonings
   ²/₃ cup water
   1 can (16 ounces) refried beans, warmed

TOPPINGS
   Shredded lettuce and cheese, chopped tomatoes

Preheat oven to 400°F. Cut each tortilla into quarters, forming 4 triangles. Place triangles in a single layer on a baking sheet. Brush each side of triangle lightly with oil. Bake for 4 to 5 minutes or until golden brown and crispy; let cool. Meanwhile, in large skillet, brown ground pork over medium high heat until crumbly, drain fat. Stir in Taco Spices & Seasonings and water. Bring to a boil; reduce heat to low and cook, uncovered for 7 minutes, stirring occasionally. To assemble tostadas, evenly divide and spread refried beans on each tortilla triangles. Spread about ¼ cup seasoned pork on top of beans. Top with shredded lettuce, cheese and tomatoes, as desired.   *Makes 8 tostadas*

Variations: Cut each tortilla into 8 pieces and make mini appetizer tostadas. For additional toppings try — sliced black olives, sour cream, guacamole, salsa or jalapenos.

Prep. Time: 15 minutes • Cook Time: 16 to 18 minutes

perfect pita pizzas

  2 whole wheat or white pita bread rounds
  ½ cup spaghetti or pizza sauce
  ¾ cup (3 ounces) shredded part-skim mozzarella cheese
  1 small zucchini, sliced ¼ inch thick
  ½ small carrot, peeled and sliced
  2 cherry tomatoes, halved
  ¼ small green bell pepper, sliced

1. Preheat oven to 375°F. Line baking sheet with foil; set aside.

2. Using small scissors, carefully split each pita around edge; separate to form 2 rounds.

3. Place rounds, rough sides up, on prepared baking sheet. Bake 5 minutes.

4. Spread 2 tablespoons spaghetti sauce onto each round; sprinkle with cheese. Decorate with vegetables to create faces. Bake 10 to 12 minutes or until cheese melts.

Makes 4 servings

Pepperoni Pita Pizzas: Prepare pita rounds, partially bake and top with spaghetti sauce and cheese as directed. Place 2 small pepperoni slices on each pizza for eyes. Decorate with cut-up fresh vegetables for rest of face. Continue to bake as directed.

perfect pita pizzas

chunky joes

Nonstick cooking spray
1 pound 95% lean ground beef
1½ cups finely chopped green bell pepper
1 can (14½ ounces) stewed tomatoes
¼ cup water
2 tablespoons tomato paste
1 tablespoon chili powder
1 tablespoon Worcestershire sauce
1 packet sugar substitute
1 teaspoon ground cumin, divided
6 hamburger buns, warmed

1. Lightly coat 12-inch skillet with cooking spray. Heat over high heat until hot. Add beef; cook and stir 3 minutes or until no longer pink. Drain on paper towels; set aside. Wipe out skillet with paper towel.

2. Coat skillet with cooking spray; heat over medium-high heat until hot. Add beef, bell pepper; cook and stir 4 minutes or until bell pepper is just tender. Add tomatoes, water, tomato paste, chili powder, Worcestershire, sugar substitute and ½ teaspoon cumin. Bring to a boil. Reduce heat and simmer, covered, 20 minutes or until thickened.

3. Remove from heat and stir in remaining ½ teaspoon cumin. If thicker consistency is desired, cook 5 minutes longer, uncovered, stirring frequently.

4. Spoon ½ cup mixture onto each bun.

Makes 6 servings

Acknowledgments

The publisher would like to thank the companies and organizations listed below for the use of their recipes and photographs in this publication.

Birds Eye® Foods

Bob Evans®

Cherry Marketing Institute

Chilean Fresh Fruit Association

Dole Food Company, Inc.

Eagle Brand® Sweetened Condensed Milk

Egg Beaters®

Equal® sweetener

The Golden Grain Company®

Hershey Foods Corporation

Hillshire Farm®

Hormel Foods, LLC

Hostess®

JOLLY TIME® Pop Corn

Lawry's® Foods

© Mars, Incorporated 2004

MASTERFOODS USA

National Honey Board

Nestlé USA

Reckitt Benckiser Inc.

The J.M. Smucker Company

Sun•Maid® Growers of California

Texas Peanut Producers Board

Unilever Bestfoods North America

Index

Index

Index

Index